Establishing Ombudsman Offices:
Recent Experience in the United States

INSTITUTE OF GOVERNMENTAL STUDIES
University of California, Berkeley

JK
9349
. O4
846
1971
WEST

Establishing Ombudsman Offices: Recent Experience in the United States

Transcript of the Ombudsman Workshop.
Honolulu, Hawaii   May 5–7, 1971

STANLEY V. ANDERSON and JOHN E. MOORE, Editors
Department of Political Science
University of California, Santa Barbara

1972

A publication of the Institute's Ombudsman Activities Project,
funded by the Office of Economic Opportunity Grant Number CG-9041

LIBRARY OF CONGRESS CATALOGING IN PUBLICATION DATA

Ombudsman Workshop, Honolulu, 1971.
  Establishing ombudsman offices.

  Includes bibliographical references.
  1. Ombudsman--Hawaii--Congresses. 2. Ombudsman--
United States--Congresses. I. Anderson, Stanley V., ed.
II. Moore, John E., 1928-   ed. III. California.
University. Institute of Governmental Studies.
IV. Title
JK9349.04046 1971   353.9'969'0091   72-5772
ISBN 0-87772-154-8

$3.00

This volume is
affectionately dedicated to
PROFESSOR STEPHAN HURWITZ
  pioneer Danish Ombudsman
  and world ambassador

FOREWORD

For nearly ten years, the Institute of Governmental Studies
has been aiding, encouraging and publishing the results of research
on the treatment of citizens' complaints and the roles of Ombudsman-
like institutions. In 1970, these efforts were greatly augmented by
the creation of the Institute's Ombudsman Activities Project and its
funding by the U.S. Office of Economic Opportunity. Professor Stanley
V. Anderson of the University's Santa Barbara campus, one of the
nation's leading pioneers in Ombudsman research, is the project
director.

The Ombudsman Activities Project has proven most timely: Recent
developments appear to presage an Ombudsman "wave of the future" in
the United States and throughout the world. Interest has intensified
in methods of improving citizen-government communication and understanding, as well as removing sources of civic discontent with the
behavior and performance of governmental bureaucracies.

Variations on the Scandinavian-originated Ombudsman appear to be
peculiarly effective in achieving these objectives. Such institutions are widely accepted as having demonstrated their worth in the
eyes of both citizens and government officials in many jurisdictions,
principally outside the United States. They are being experimented
with--or their establishment is being contemplated--in many other
areas.

The period of experimentation is now well under way in the
United States. The present volume--the first published fruit of the

Ombudsman Activities Project--attempts to distill the principal findings of these initial Ombudsman efforts. Taking the form of a Working Paper, this document presents a nearly verbatim report of a workshop conducted in Hawaii, May 5-7, 1971. Despite its informal tone and appearance, the volume is a major source of information and insight. It is a compendium of ideas and experience garnered by knowledgeable participants through their efforts in helping to create--and observe--several fledgling Ombudsman offices.

Appropriately, the workshop concentrated much of its attention on Hawaii, which became the Union's first state to establish an Ombudsman office. In addition, the group also drew upon the background provided by a number of other Ombudsman offices or Ombudsman-like institutions in various parts of the country.

The report deals with most of the questions that will be confronting new Ombudsmen: How to get the office going expeditiously and with the right foot forward; how to obtain necessary publicity without being inundated by complaints; how to deal with officialdom smoothly but effectively; how to handle inquiries and keep adequate records; and finally, how to answer the crucial questions, "What should we be doing, and how well are we accomplishing it?" This volume presents the pragmatic experience of some of the nation's best informed experts and participants in Ombudsman work. Accordingly, the Institute of Governmental Studies is pleased to make it available in this form for public use.

Stanley Scott
Assistant Director

TABLE OF CONTENTS

PREFACE

There are many good reasons for visiting Hawaii, but few that could be considered obligatory. Although their wives and employers might not always see it that way, Hawaii created such an obligation for students and practitioners of American Ombudsman activities when it established the first state Ombudsman office. Since the effectiveness of that office appears to depend as much on the context in which it is located as on the characteristics of the office and the qualities of the man who occupies it, the first Ombudsman Workshop drew upon a number of Hawaii's resources: In addition to its Ombudsman, Herman Doi, conference participants included members of the State Legislature, officials from state and local administrative agencies, and representatives of related complaint-handling offices.

As indicated by the title of this transcript, the conference focused on problems associated with establishing American Ombudsman offices. While Hawaii provided the principal laboratory for examining the procedures and impact of a practicing Ombudsman, the experience of successful sponsors of Ombudsman legislation in Nebraska and Seattle/ King County permitted some comparison of the circumstances of enactment in these three jurisdictions. Similarly, the experience of Honolulu's Office of Information and Complaint afforded opportunities to compare the characteristics of a local executive "ombudsman" with those of a state office patterned after the Scandinavian prototype. The latter comparison was particularly pointed, as the two offices share jurisdiction over the City and County of Honolulu.

The conference consisted of five half-day sessions, beginning on May 5 and ending on May 7, 1971. As indicated in each of the following sections, its composition varied somewhat from one session to the next. The participants were:

Ira Kaye and Patricia Stolfa, both of the Office of Program Development, U.S. Office of Economic Opportunity;

Professors Stanley Anderson, John Moore and Alan Wyner, and Research Assistant Albert Liston, all of the University of California, Santa Barbara;

Speaker of the House Tadao Beppu and Senator Duke Kawasaki, both of the Hawaii State Legislature;

Senator Loran Schmit of the Nebraska State Legislature;

City Councilman Liem Tuai, Seattle, Washington;

Hawaii State Ombudsman Herman S. Doi;

Ombudsman-designate Leland Walton, Seattle/King County;

University of Hawaii Ombudsman Charles James;

Philip Douglas, Office of the Mayor, Newark, New Jersey;

James Loomis, Director, and Patrick De Costa, Assistant Director for Complaints, Honolulu Office of Information and Complaints;

Ralph Kondo, Director, Department of Taxation, State of Hawaii; and

Deputy Chief Charles Duarte, Honolulu Police Department.

The experience related herein confirms several expectations that have been conventionally associated with the Ombudsman office, and suggests the need to revise certain others to fit the American context. While generalizations about American Ombudsman offices would certainly be premature, experience to date indicates that:

(1) Both the classical model and executive-branch variations on the Ombudsman theme are capable of resolving individual grievances,

forestalling recurrent complaints, and exonerating public officials of unfounded criticism. However, complaint-handling by Executive Ombudsmen is more dependent upon the commitment of the chief executive to this activity, and weaker in its ability to exonerate administrative personnel in the absence of complementary (and presumably independent) grievance mechanisms, such as newspaper action-lines;

(2) For all the efforts that may be made to assure the independence of "proper" Ombudsman offices, they remain significantly dependent upon the legislative body that appropriates their funds, and upon auxiliary grievance mechanisms for handling complaints that fall outside their jurisdiction or that would overtax their limited resources with inquiries or requests for services that do not require the distinctive competence of an Ombudsman;

(3) Perhaps in recognition of both its ultimate dependence on legislative appropriations and the impatience of American bureaucrats with formal correspondence and recommendations, the first American Ombudsman office is much more inclined to reach informal agreements leading to "voluntary rectifications" than are its counterparts in other countries; and

(4) It appears that however successful an Ombudsman-related office may be in reaching the source of a particular set of complaints, that success will not--at least in the short run--diminish the overall volume of complaints. To the contrary, it may generate additional complaints from those who earlier saw no reason to register their grievances.

In addition to stimulating these and perhaps other generalizations, the primary purpose of the transcript is to provide a source of guidance to incipient Ombudsmen in the United States.

* * *

Everyone interested in American applications of the Ombudsman concept is indebted to the State of Hawaii for establishing the first tate Ombudsman office. The participants in this conference are further indebted to several of Hawaii's first citizens: to House Speaker Tadao Beppu and Senator Duke Kawasaki for their hospitality at the State Capitol; to Ombudsman Herman Doi for both his exemplary experience and the generosity with which he has shared it; to his secretary, Mrs. Ellen Onaga, for her help in making arrangements for the conference; and to Jim Loomis, Pat De Costa, Charlie James, Ralph Kondo and Charles Duarte for their substantial contributions to its content.

While Hawaii supplied much of the substance and all of the facilities for the conference, the U.S. Office of Economic Opportunity provided the wherewithal through its funding of the Ombudsman Activities Project. We gratefully acknowledge OEO's support, but absolve it of responsibility for the viewpoints expressed herein.

We would also like to thank Albert Liston for taping and proof-reading, and Mrs. Ellen Hays for her cheerfulness and efficiency in the laborious task of transcribing the conference tapes and typing the heavily edited final version. As we have come to expect, our colleagues in the Institute of Governmental Studies have been helpful, especially Assistant Director Stanley Scott and Administrative Assistants Hazel Karns and Joan Barulich.

Stanley Anderson
John Moore

Santa Barbara, California
June, 1972

SCOPE AND OBJECTIVES OF THE OMBUDSMAN
ACTIVITIES PROJECT

Professor Anderson:

I would like to say just a few words about the
Ombudsman Activities Project, to put our work here
in some perspective. We go back to about 1964, when
Stanley Scott, Assistant Director of the Institute of
Governmental Studies was inspired by the creation of
the new office in New Zealand. He suggested to me
that the Institute of Governmental Studies ought to
keep an eye on Ombudsman developments and follow them and
study them. And we did--initially directing our
attention to more pronounced activities in Canada.[1]
Then, we sponsored a study of complaint-handling
procedures in the California Legislature written by
Professor Dean Mann, who is also a colleague of ours on
the Santa Barbara campus at the University of California.
His paper is subtitled Complaint-Handling Procedures
of Three California Legislators, so it is quite limited,
but it is a pioneer study.[2] No major scholarly study
has ever been done on the complaint-handling procedures
of American legislators, and yet every legislator knows
what an important and time-consuming activity this is.

We also arranged for a study of mail flow in the office
of Governor Edmund Brown of California, conducted by
Professor Gerald McDaniel. It is an unpublished
study, partly incorporated in a piece by

1

John Moore in the American Assembly book,[3] and we
hope to make further use of it at some appropriate
time when we can compare it to mail flow studies in
other jurisdictions or with another Governor in
California. Our momentum picked up with the American
Assembly in 1967 at Arden House, sponsored by Columbia
University, followed half a year later by the Western
Assembly in Berkeley, which was co-sponsored by the
Institute of Governmental Studies.[4] Herman Doi was
one of the participants in that conference and we are
proud to have had him there at a time before he was
Ombudsman here.

That, as you can see, is four or five years with a
fairly modest output. But then along came the Hawaiian
Ombudsman, and I was very gratified when my colleague
John Moore made the ultimate sacrifice of coming to
live here for several months to gather data on this
important development.

Herman Doi was approaching his first anniversary when
the Office of Economic Opportunity volunteered to support
further Ombudsman projects in Iowa--where the Governor
has appointed a Citizens' Aide--in Nebraska and Seattle/

King County, and more recently in Newark, New Jersey.
With additional support from OEO, the Institute was
able to expand its studies through the Ombudsman
Activities Project. At a minimum, we want to follow
and study the Ombudsman offices supported by the Office
of Economic Opportunity, and quite obviously we will
have to keep a continuing eye on the Hawaii office,
because this is the cutting edge of Ombudsman
developments in America. Herman Doi will be facing
problems a year, two or three ahead of other Ombudsmen;
it would be foolish for us not to take advantage of
his experience and his imaginative way of coping with
the problems which inevitably crop up.

In addition to the Ombudsman offices supported by OEO,
we have been carrying out some other studies.
Professor Dean Mann has gathered the data for a study
of the Pennsylvania Governor's Branch Offices. These
provide a way for complaint mechanisms to reach out
to potential clients. The Governor established about
20 of these offices, including one mobile unit. With
a change of parties the new Governor has evidently
decided to dismantle them, and instead, quite interest-
ingly, to give about $10,000 additional staff support
to every state legislator --trying to beef up the complaint-

handling function of the legislators. Frankly, I think that is just fine in its own right, but is not really a substitute for the other approach. Hopefully, as we shall see in the course of this conference, there is need for both activities.

Professor Alan Wyner is studying Executive Ombudsmen. Lt. Governor Mark Hogan had set himself up as an Ombudsman in Colorado, with very limited staff. Every time he got any publicity he was swamped. We have been able to get some material on that. And then in Illinois, the Lt. Governor is carrying out an active complaint-handling function, and we understand that now the New Mexico Lt. Governor has been officially designated a complaint handler, so we hope that these three Lt. Governors' efforts will permit us to get a well-rounded study of this particular form.[5]

It turned out, as Alan Wyner and I went to Chicago, that there was a fascinating battery of complaint mechanisms there. We initially thought we would be studying the State of Illinois, but I think now we will probably concentrate on Chicago, because you have there the Governor's Branch Offices--there are three

of them in Chicago--and as just mentioned, the Lt.
Governor is quite active. Then, the Mayor has an
Office of Information and Inquiry which is very active,
and has been for many years. Finally, we found
hidden under the title of Registrar of Citizens' Complaints a Civilian Police Review Board. This is a
study which Alan Wyner has well under way, and that
will be included in a book he is editing on Executive
Ombudsmen in America. Well, this is the long and the
short of what we are doing, which brings us to this
particular conference.

THE FIRST ANNUAL OMBUDSMAN WORKSHOP

This conference was planned on rather short notice
for reasons which were beyond our control. Mainly,
we wanted to have a conference for the new Ombudsmen
and the legislators primarily responsible for initia-
ting the idea, because we feel that one important
aspect of the Ombudsman office is the relationship of
the office to the legislators. There is a need for
key legislators to be very familiar with the workings of
these offices, so they can cooperate with them, help
shape them, and do the things required to make the
Ombudsman office more effective. But it was a cliff-

hanger, because we didn't know just when the appointments would be made in Seattle and Nebraska. Very
happily, as you know, the appointment was made in
Seattle. Senator Schmit is holding us in suspense on
an appointment in Nebraska. Frankly, I hope that
this is/ the first annual Ombudsman workshop. Not that
            only
we will necessarily follow the same format another
time, but perhaps a year from now, maybe in Santa
Barbara, maybe in one of the places where there is an
American Ombudsman, we will bring the Ombudsmen
together and perhaps include those in Canada, whose
experiences, I think, would be very valuable.

There has been a tradition of Ombudsmen touching base
with one another when they are appointed, going to
Scandinavia and perhaps to the Canadian Provinces.
Herman Doi was one who did this, among others, and I
think it is a very valuable experience. But one can
see that if the number of Ombudsmen increase, this
is going to be an increasingly cumbersome chore, and
ultimately the Ombudsmen will have to become very
selective, and not be able to go to all of them.
Rather than each Ombudsman making a circuit, why not
bring them all together, say once a year, and let
them share their experiences in workshops which focus

on specific problems of setting up and running an
Ombudsman office? So the focus of this particular,
this first annual Ombudsman workshop--we have now
established a tradition--is on problems of commencing
operation.

We are not really going back to the very beginning of
this topic at this conference, because we are not
studying the politics of enactment of an Ombudsman
bill, where at least three of the participants here
could undoubtedly spend a half a day each telling us
of the politics of having gotten their bill through the
legislature. I am struck by the fact that two of the
successful proponents were freshman Senators, and
by the fact that while there have been bills introduced
in roughly two-thirds, approaching three-quarters, of
the American states, that the two that have gotten
through, and the one in Seattle, have gotten through
on the first time around. They haven't been bills
which were in for a year and then put aside and then
taken up again. Some initial momentum carried them
through and they didn't lapse into the limbo that other
Ombudsman legislation has in other states.

But, as indicated, we are not talking about the politics

of enactment. Nor are we talking on a comparative basis about the general structure of Ombudsman offices, though I think a mention of the particular, peculiar nature of the Seattle office is in order, because it embodies two "firsts." It is the first municipal Ombudsman. There are other Ombudsmen who have jurisdiction over local Government, in Scandinavia and elsewhere, but they are also Ombudsmen for a state, or a province or a country. There are people sometimes called local Ombudsmen, who are really Executive Ombudsmen, who work as an aide to a chief executive of a city or county, and they do not have the independence which characterizes an Ombudsman. So, the Seattle Ombudsman is the first solely local government, classical-type Ombudsman in the world.

Also, Seattle and King County have made the first joint appointment of an Ombudsman. As we turn a little later to our three legislators who are going to tell us about the problems of selecting an Ombudsman, perhaps Councilman Tuai will comment on the double pro- blem of having to secure the support of two different legislative bodies. Yet, it may very well be worth the price, in that you are covering what people per- ceive as the real unit of government. They do not go around identifying which unit of government they have come into contact with. They want a solution to their problems, and this is a way of bridging these more or less artificial jurisdictional lines. One of the peculiarities of the Ombudsman office is that, because the Ombudsman has no coercive power, the normal problems of defining jurisdiction are not as important as they would be, for example, for a court, so that it is quite appropriate that the Ombudsman office have a double jurisdiction. (I suppose in the interests of precision I ought to mention that the first British Parliamentary Commissioner for Administration/, who (P.C.A.) receives complaints only from members of Parliament, did serve both the House of Commons in London, and the Stormont in Northern Ireland. I would have to enter into a lengthy argument as to whether the P.C.A. is in fact an Ombudsman--in some ways it is, and in other ways it isn't.) So those are Seattle's two firsts--the joint appointment of an Ombudsman in municipal government.

Then, too, we are not treating with Executive Ombudsmen at any great length here, although we will have an opportunity to relate the Ombudsman to other offices tomorrow, and among these offices will be complaint officials connected with executive agencies.

John Moore, the gentleman who arranged this meeting--
with the assistance of the Ombudsman office here in
Hawaii--has prepared an outline for us which, as I
look at it, suggests sections of a booklet of instructions
on how to set up an Ombudsman office. And if you look
at it you will see that this morning we are talking
about selecting American Ombudsmen, the problem of
choosing, not the right man, but a right man to do the
job. This afternoon John Moore is going to put the
Ombudsman office into the context of other agencies of
appeal that are available to the people of Hawaii for
making complaints. Then Herman Doi is going to
present us with his view of the steps to be taken
in setting up an office. In his usual efficient manner,
Mr. Doi has prepared some materials which will assist
him in making that presentation. Then tomorrow, we
will be dealing with relationships with complementary
offices--the Legislature, City and County offices,
the University Ombudsman--and in the afternoon with
respondant agencies--taxation and the police. So I
think in the course of going through this agenda, we
will have pretty much covered all the major problems
that an Ombudsman faces in initially setting up his
office.

Next year, perhaps, we will shift the focus; we will take problems that any Ombudsman would have with a going office. So we now finally reach the topic of this morning session, which is How to Choose an Ombudsman.

SELECTING AMERICAN OMBUDSMEN

Someday, we are going to have a bad Ombudsman, or several, because I think this institution is going to become garden variety. When it does, somebody, somewhere, is going to appoint an Ombudsman who really, for one reason or another, cannot do the job. By then, the institution of Ombudsman will be able to tolerate that. People will see it not as a reflection on the idea of the office, but simply that this particular person was unable to carry it out. Right now we need all good ones, because people are not only judging the individual, they are judging the office. And I say very fortunately we have been extremely lucky, especially in our very first Ombudsman. I know that Herman Doi does not want this conference to become simply an encomium to him, so I won't amplify that at this point, anyway. And the next two or three, four, five or six are also going to be extremely important, although the incremental importance will diminish as the success of the initial ones becomes evident.

11

What people seem to want in choosing an Ombudsman is
some kind of an immaculate conception. They want some
device to precipitate out an ideal person who fits
the job. First of all, there is no such person. There
are many different personality types and backgrounds
that would make a good Ombudsman and there are some
working conditions that will foster the operation of
the office, and some which will not. So, as I mentioned before, we are only looking for a good man, and--
again quite obviously--what you need is some way to
ensure that you know about qualified applicants and
have some way then of carefully screening those
applicants.

GENERAL CRITERIA

What are the qualities of a good Ombudsman? You will
all have a chance to pick at my categories later on.
What about age, for example?

The Ombudsmen up to, I would say, Herman Doi, have
generally been people in the later years   of middle
age or the beginning of old age. In Denmark, Professor
Stephan Hurwitz, for example, took over at 55. He was
able to serve for sixteen years, and now he is stepping
down. The man who is replacing him is in his early

12

forties. Fifty-five was good because it gave Hurwitz
a chance to put his mark on the office, gave him time
to travel, as he did, and to circularize the idea.

The very first Ombudsman, Mannerheim in Sweden, back
in 1810, was a very political appointee. He had
been a prominent political personality, and it took him
a couple of decades to iron the political aspect out
of it, and to establish it as a non-political judicial-
type of office. Today, the Scandinavian countries often
appoint judges. In Norway, for example, you have a
retired judge. In Finland and Sweden, civil servants
get a civil service status under which they can become
an Ombudsman and go back to their other job without any
difficulty. So it tends to become a step on the way
to a prominent judicial career. In other words, the
Ombudsman post is one segment of being a clerk in a
court, a subordinate judge, a regular judge, and
eventually an appeal judge, and so on. We just do
not operate that way in this hemisphere.

The New Zealand Ombudsman, again, was retired. A
vigorous man, he has been in office since 1962, and
so he has had time to make a mark.

I am suggesting, then, that age is not a crucial factor. Conceivably, you could have Ombudsmen who are quite young. Someday, it seems to me, you are going to have Ombudsmen for jurisdictions of rather small size and population, with consequent budgetary limitations. I think you will have, just as with young city managers, an Ombudsman at a lower salary in a small town. His route to promotion is to get recognition and to move on to larger and more difficult assignments. Someday we will have young and not enormously highly paid Ombudsmen.

At any age, the person chosen should be vigorous and be able to serve at least three, four, five or six years, in order to really get the office off to a good start. Now, this is not a universal rule. Maybe you can have a stop-gap first appointee who just sort of keeps the thing going for a year or two, and then later bring in a person who will take off from there and build the office up. But, ideally, I think you should get someone right off the bat who not only will be energetic and enthusiastic, but will have enough time to get the office started, because he will certainly define its personality.

Canada, too, has chosen mostly retired persons, a
retired law professor, a retired university president,
and a retired Commissioner of the Royal Canadian
Mounted Police. The one I have met of those is an
extremely vigorous gentleman in Alberta, the former
Royal Canadian Mounted Commissioner.

What about sex? Frankly, I just do not see any
reason why women wouldn't make good Ombudsmen--the
right woman, just as it has to be the right man. And
I don't think we should build in any kind of a subtle
restriction of sex, in selecting and appointing people
to this office. In fact, I would rather think we should
actively seek out qualified women for this work. A
tradition once established may indeed make it one of
the occupations which it is permissible under our mores
for a woman to hold.

What about law-training? Again, in Scandinavia, not
only are the Ombudsmen lawyers, or judges, but the
Constitution or law even requires that they must have
had legal training. In New Zealand, it is true that
they chose a lawyer, but not a gentleman who had
been a practicing lawyer. Rather, it was one who had
been a soldier during the Second World War, a diplomat--

15

and therefore a civil servant--and then the last High Commissioner in Samoa, helping lead it to independence. So I don't think that the fact that Sir Guy Powles was a lawyer was the primary consideration in his choice; rather, it was the totality of his background.

When we move to Canada, we see that we are getting away from the exclusive appointment of lawyers and judges to this office. The one in Quebec is former Dean of the law school at Laval University, so he is certainly a lawyer. But the other two are not, although one has had a life-long connection with the law. In New Brunswick, Dr. Ross Flemington was a retired University President. Of course, he has access to legal advice when he needs it. Then, in Alberta, the fact that the Ombudsman there was Commissioner of the Mounted Police certainly gave him a familiarity with the law. His top deputy is a lawyer, and is able to give him the legal advice that he needs in carrying out his work.

Herman Doi, of course, is a lawyer, and I don't think we should exclude lawyers from the profession. And now, in Seattle, Lee Walton comes from a career in city management. So, again, I think a law background can be useful, but I don't think a person who doesn't have a specific law background should be excluded.

Let me put this into a broader context. I think the
era of the monopoly of law practiced by certified
lawyers is ending in this country, and we are moving
towards para-professionals. We are recognizing that
real estate brokers and others conduct legal activity
and rather than just ignoring it and pretending that
the lawyers have a total monopoly, it is time that we
should recognize that Ombudsman work is a specialized
kind of legal work. A lawyer who has had three years
of law school and a vast experience is only going to
be able to use a certain segment of that. In Herman
Doi's case, for example, the fact that he has been
Director of the Legislative Reference Bureau was an
important segment of his experience for being effective
in this job. Being a lawyer is one factor we should
take into account, but its absence should not exclude
a person from consideration.

In the Buffalo experiment, everybody was a lawyer, or
a law student, and as a political scientist and a
lawyer I feel somewhat chagrined that the political
scientists have not yet followed suit, because in
Buffalo, with the help of the Office of Economic

Opportunity, two professors became super-Ombudsmen, their students in seminars became middle-grade Ombudsmen, and they in turn found people in the local ghettos who were intermediary Ombudsmen.[6] For the short period of time that that project was in operation, they did a very useful job of servicing complaints in areas where poor people live. But why couldn't that be done by a Sociology Department, or a Political Science Department or by a combination of all three?

Well, so far I've established that age, sex and law training are not overwhelmingly limiting criteria. I suppose that majority would be a limitation—you would have to be an adult—but again, maybe not. Maybe in the school system we could have children of the same age as those for whom they are serving as Ombudsmen.

Now we get to an essential criterion, and that is governmental expertise. Somehow, somewhere, in the training of that person, he must have gotten to know how government works. My own feeling is—and this is almost a contradiction in terms—that the Ombudsman has to be a general expert. He has to be an expert in government, not in some narrow focus, but more generally in the

overview of government. And I think this is a kind
of overview that you get by, say, working in a
Legislative Reference Bureau. So the question I want
to raise is, must that expertise, even though it may
be general, must it relate to the specific area where
the Ombudsman is going to function? In other words,
does the man who becomes Ombudsman in New Jersey, does
he have to know New Jersey politicans, New Jersey
political history, or can he fill in the concrete
details on the basis of his previous general understanding of the way government works in America?

To put it in local terms, in Hawaii for example, I
don't think a Malahini could have done the job. For
those of you who don't know, a "Malahini" is a newcomer.
Why is that? I may be wrong in this, and I would
appreciate discussion on it later, but I think that
the fabric of social life and politics in Hawaii is
so unique that to bring an outsider in here would
be very cruel. You wouldn't want to send the kid up
in a crate like that, because it would take him so
long to get his feet back on the ground. He would
not be able to transpose his general governmental
familiarity from the Mainland to the very special
characteristics of Hawaii. I am exaggerating for

purposes of emphasis.

But in Seattle, on the other hand, the search for an Ombudsman was not limited to Seattleites, to King Countyers, or to Washingtonians, but was nationwide. What are the pros and cons of limiting your choice to your own area and going nationwide? Well, I think that the limitation in Hawaii is one that should only be used in places where the local situation is such that an outsider would not be able to function for a considerable period of time.

Let me go on to the polar opposite. One can make the argument that an Ombudsman ought always to come from outside the jurisdiction where he is serving. That way, he avoids any burden of past connections. In other words, his independence and impartiality will be buttressed by the fact that he is simply not identified with any party, or faction or group in the State or City where he serves. Frankly, I think this is probably the case in New Jersey, that you would want a person to come in who was free from any implication of past associations.

We are going to hear about the experience in Nebraska.

But I wonder, does the person who becomes Ombudsman
in Nebraska have to be a Nebraskan? Or would it be
better to cast a wider net. You might end up with
someone from Nebraska, but you would make your selection
on some basis other than local residence.

Turning to another characteristic of a good Ombudsman,
he has to be independent. This is simply a definition
of the job. This is why Executive Ombudsmen are not
true Ombudsmen. They may approach it on a spectrum,
on a continuum. As the Ombudsman who works for, say,
the Governor of Oregon, or the Governor of Iowa, or
for some Mayor, as his chief executive directs and
orders that Ombudsman to be independent, so he will
be, and then the problem is to convince other
people that he is, so that this aura of independence
and objectivity will be appreciated.

It will never be completely successful, because, just
as with justice, it must be seen to be done, as well
as done. So there is always the suspicion and the stigma
of being an employee of the man whose other employees
you are investigating that somehow you may not be telling
it like it is. But, I merely bring this in to emphasize
the complete independence of the Ombudsman which is a

very remarkable characteristic of that office.
Obviously, he should not have a political hue which
is unmistakable;   he should have an appearance of
nonpartisanship.

No one, probably, is without some political association.
Everyone has voted, they have registered, they may even
as good citizens have participated in politics. But
you all know that you reach a point of identification
where you are known as a leader, an active and
professional politican of a certain party, and I think
this is why most Ombudsman statutes have cooling-off
periods. You cannot have been, say, a councilman,
or a state legislator, for a number of years before
you assume the job of Ombudsman.

Now I'm getting to the last characteristic, and I
saved the hardest one for the end, and that is
temperament. This is what we are really talking about.
What kind of a person, what kind of a personality
makes a good Ombudsman? A good listener, we have
heard, yes. He has to be willing to listen to everyone,
and there are many people who just don't like to listen,
who are impatient. So you want a person who listens
patiently. But when you listen patiently and you

have heard a story once or twice, that doesn't
mean you are obligated to hear it a third or fourth
or fifth time.

In any event, as I have already intimated, the person
is not a paragon of virtue. That is, you are not
looking for a saint when you are seeking an Ombudsman.
I don't think a saint could do the job. Saints are
for preaching, for inspiring, for changing basic mores.
An Ombudsman is for making sure that the going
commonality of values is actually enforced, the rules
of law and the accepted moral standards of that
community are actually applied in individual cases.
He may improve them just a bit over time, and so
have an impact on moral standards, but his primary
job is not to attack the standards by attempting to
overturn them or revolutionize them and make
drastic changes in them. He is a man of his times,
with the feelings and the conflicts that anyone else
has, and that is why he can sympathize with the
complainant, and with the civil servants whom he is
investigating. Beyond the qualities of being willing
to listen, and able to project this receptivity, there
is a quality of humanity that appreciates the
ambivalences of human action, rather than attempting

to impose some pure notion of virtue.

Finally, an Ombudsman needs what we will have to call
a judicious temperament, that is, the qualities of
the judge: the man who listens, weighs carefully,
makes sure that he has all the facts, and then reaches
a judgment. So, he is a man of action in the sense
that he does conclude this process with some "yes"
or "no," and not just with a scratch of the head and
a, "Well, I don't know, maybe yes, or maybe no."
This requires him then to be astute and persistent in
his work.

I am sure we can all feel the qualities more than
these verbal expressions of them, and so what is really
important is how to find this man. We need some
mechanism, and that is what our other speakers today
are going to be telling us about. How cumbersome a
mechanism do you need, or how simple a one can you have?
My own feeling is that while an Executive Ombudsman can
be easily appointed by administrative fiat, and the
mayor or governor who appoints him may be a very good
man, I am not satisfied with the simplicity of that
process. I think that any single individual should
not trust his own judgment so far as to say, 'there's

the Ombudsman, I appoint him.'

I began this presentation by noting there are two
steps involved here. One is getting applications to
come in--how to solicit them, how to publicize the
availability of the job. This is where the issue of
whether you are going to be locally oriented, or
whether you are going to go statewide or nationwide is important. Then I think you need a further
two-step process after that; the screening and
appointing process should be separated. You need a
legitimizing body to eliminate people who are obviously
not qualified, and then to make that hard judgment of
ranking people who are qualified, coming up with a
list of one, two, three or whatever it is, with the
appointing body then being required to ratify that
decision. Well these are perfectly obvious remarks
I'm making. It is sometimes embarrassing to put oneself
out as an expert. I have finally decided that an
expert is someone who is well grounded in the obvious.

I guess the last category here would be how to keep a
qualified Ombudsman. I'm very happy to say that the
turnover in Ombudsman offices is very slow. People
seem to like the work. As I mentioned, Hurwitz is now

finishing about 15 years in that office. Sir Guy
Powles has been in office since 1962. The long tenure,
especially of initial Ombudsmen, is a valuable
thing. To keep them you want to treat them right, and
there are many different ways that you can do that.
So, I end with my own little sermon to legislators,
but those who are here have not only tried to keep
good Ombudsmen, but have been responsible for getting
them in the first place.

SPECIFIC APPLICATIONS

Hawaii

Senator Kawasaki:
I want you to know that I am heartily in favor of your
having annual seminars on the Ombudsman, and I just
hope that you won't forget to notify the President of
the Senate who makes all the assignments.

I think there was no one as well qualified as Herman
Doi for the position here in Hawaii. There was
resistance to the whole concept to begin with. This
is something quite new and revolutionary around here,
so it was important that everybody in the Legislature
knew Herman's work. He was, as mentioned previously,
Director of the Legislative Reference Bureau. He

also served as a Deputy Attorney General on contract to that office in past years. He was chief clerk of the House Finance Committee for a session or two. He had also published a number of papers on governmental processes and procedures, all of which is to say that his background was very familiar to the members of the Legislature of both parties, and he was at one time or the other consulted by every member of the Legislature on bills that a legislator wanted drafted. They knew the quality of his work, and they knew his temperament. Stan mentioned the temperament that is required of this position. I'll tell you that Herman's low key posture really helped contribute to the unanimous confirmation of his appointment: 24 votes in the Senate of the 25 (one was excused), 48 in the House. We provide in our bill that the appointment be by majority vote of both Houses sitting in joint session, and this is what took place on April 17, 1969.

So, as I said, we had no problem. We went through the usual procedures of having hearings, asking for applicants, and we had a whole gamut of people applying for this position. We had a man apply who is right now the leading ecologist around here. He's

been campaigning ever since he failed to make the
U.S. Senate race in last year's election. We had
the University of Hawaii President, Thomas Hamilton,
who has now left that position, who was also interested
in the Ombudsman Office--except that he heard that a man
who had worked under him, as the Director of the
Reference Bureau, was also interested. He figured
that he didn't have the kind of rapport that Herman
Doi had with the legislators, so he immediately took
himself out. We had exmilitary intelligence people.
We also had a woman who was Chairman, or Mayor, of one
of the outer island counties who was interested,
Mrs. Helene Hale. I felt that she was qualified.
But frankly, any other name, other than Herman Doi's
name, would never have been confirmed. So, we had
it very easy, and I trust that some of the other
states will find a man as eminently qualified as
Herman.

We had no problem in selecting the man for that
position, because Herman Doi was so far better qualified
than anybody else who applied. And, incidentally,
that point that you made, Stan, that a Malahini or a
newcomer here would not have fared so well here is
very true, because I don't think we could have gotten

anywhere close to a majority vote if it was a newcomer.
I think the boys here are pretty reluctant to appoint
someone who was not familiar with the policies
of government here, and did not know the personalities
involved. This is important both on the county
level and the state level: the legislators, and
administrators, the government department heads, and
the agency heads. So, the fact that he was a local
boy, who had an excellent background, who did work for
every member of the Legislature here, this helped.
As a matter of fact, I might say that if it wasn't
for the fact that Herman generally was considered as
the chief candidate for the position of the Ombudsman,
I don't think even the enabling legislation providing
for the office would have been passed. This is how
important a part a single personality played on the
legislation. This is the primary reason why the
Ombudsman act passed. In the first place, everyone
knew that the bill itself was authored by Herman Doi,
as I have told many people, because he came out with a
paper on the Ombudsman which influenced me, which
influenced many people who took the trouble to read
about the Ombudsman concept. Herman came out with that
paper back in 1965.[7] So everybody around here was of
the opinion that this was the foremost authority on

the Ombudsman position here in the State of Hawaii,
and all of these things added up to a final appointment
of Herman.

So far as the salary goes, I had suggested originally
that it be comparable to the compensation of the Chief
Justice of the Supreme Court, which at that time was
about $28,000, on the grounds that this is the kind
of thinking that went on in the Scandinavian countries:
you want to attract the best man you can find and
give him enough security and tenure to make qualified
people want to apply for this position. We had to
cut that down, as one of the compromises before the
final bill was passed. Some people in the Legislature
objected to such a high salary. They thought it
should be comparable to the compensation for a
cabinet position, which at that time was $22,000.
And this is what we settled for. Subsequently, we
did amend that bill, so that his compensation right
now is comparable to a Judge of the Circuit Court, with
comparable tenure, and so forth.

Mr. Kaye:
Is there a legislative review committee, a watch-
dog committee that in a sense is helping to evaluate
the Ombudsman institution, or is there any kind of

special review of Ombudsman procedures themselves?

Senator Kawasaki:

No, we haven't provided that machinery in the form of
a resolution or legislation, but the annual report that
Herman's office will have to make to us I suppose
would indicate to us the manner in which the office is
operated.

Ombudsman Walton:

I was just going to ask the Senator, but maybe Herman
could respond: You came out of the so-called establishment. Has this been a factor at all; has there been
any criticism that you are one of theirs?

Ombudsman Doi:

I don't think so.

Senator Kawasaki:

Maybe I can answer that. I don't think the Legislative
Reference Bureau was ever identified as partisan.

Mr. Kaye:

Well, you mentioned that he had been clerk of a legislative committee. Now that's usually appointed by the
majority party, for example. But you were not really
associated with either party?

Ombudsman Doi:
I was and I am.

Senator Kawasaki
Well, I won't say that, because he was a Democratic

appointee, and it was no secret that he was a Democrat.

Ombudsman Walton:
Has this ever come back to haunt you? You have been
able to establish your independence then in the public's
eye?

Ombudsman Doi:
I was still a Democrat while I was the Director of the
Legislative Reference Bureau, but we service both
Republicans and Democrats.

Senator Kawasaki:
That helped.

Ombudsman Walton:
It probably has to do with his personal credibility.

Professor Anderson:
Which leads to my comment, which is really just to
emphasize something that Senator Kawasaki said.
Certainly in choosing an Ombudsman you have to choose
someone who is appointable. It would be silly to
pick a man you thought was ideal if you knew ahead
of time that you couldn't get him through. But, wasn't
it to a great extent the fact that Herman Doi had the
qualities of a good Ombudsman that made him appointable?

Nebraska

Professor Moore:
Loran, in turning now to you, I suppose we might note
that there is a natural bridge, because I believe the

question of salary has been a very salient item in the process of appointing an Ombudsman in Nebraska.

Senator Schmit:

First of all, the intrigue that went on in Senator Kawasaki's area made me feel a little more at ease about the manipulations that go on in our own unique Nebraska unicameral. In Nebraska, it would have been very difficult to have passed this type of legislation if we had had a two-house system, because we are very suspicious of new agencies of government in Nebraska, and whereas your bill became law with a substantial majority, our bill just squeaked by: just a bare minimum of 25 votes out of 49 members.

I am going to speak primarily about the manner of the selection, because I think our problem differed from yours in that when legislation was introduced there was no one on the scene who could fill the job. The concept of an Ombudsman was an unfamiliar one.

The problem was, first, passing the legislation and, secondly, establishing a salary for the Ombudsman and a budget for the office. In the legislation we had set it up so that the five-man Executive Board of the Legislative Council would have to nominate him. The

previous (1969-1970) Executive Board did not approve
of the office. On the present Executive Board, only two
of the five members had supported the bill. I have
sort of a persecution complex. I felt they were trying
to do by executive order what they could not do on the
floor. In any case, they were not going to rush right
out and make a nomination.

However, we did have a man who was very well qualified
and who was interested in the position. He worked for
a Senator in Washington, and had been a statehouse
newspaper reporter for ten years. He was well known
to a vast majority of the members of the unicameral,
and was very much interested in coming back to
Nebraska to take the job of Ombudsman. Well, the
new Governor of Nebraska is a Democrat, and there was
some animosity between his office and that of the
Senator. The Governor, who is a friend of mine,
although he is a member of the other party, expressed
to me his concern that this man would come back from
Washington and use the office of Ombudsman for the
purpose of promoting the Senator's reelection. I
assured him that I was sure this would not happen
and he took my word for it. Then, one of the
candidate's closest friends in the unicameral sent a

34

letter around to the members of the legislature endorsing the nomination, in the hope of prodding the Executive Board into making the nomination. He got 37 signatures on this letter without even contacting any of the five members of the Executive Board, so I was rather relaxed and thought things were going well. The Executive Board felt a little trapped by this action of the body but they were not going to let it affect their wisdom, they told me.

Then the roof fell in. The Governor came out with a strong statement endorsing him, prior to the action of the Executive Board. Well, this was almost too much for the Board to take. They just sat tight for a few days. Then the matter of salary became an issue again. They said they would not pay over $18,000. With the furor that was created by the Governor's endorsement, the applicant asked that his name be withdrawn. He did so with tongue in cheek, more or less, thinking that if they really wanted him they would come back to him and say, we are not going to allow small differences to create problems and would ask him to take the job. On the other hand, he did realize what else could happen and what in fact did happen. They accepted his letter, gave it

to the press, and just like that he was out of
contention.

Because they had wanted to be fair in their approach
to the job, they had advertised through the press for
persons who were interested in the position and they had
numerous persons contact the Executive Board. They
interviewed perhaps 20 to 25 persons, all kinds of
persons. Some of them were very good, but none of
them was as good as the man that we had first
suggested for the position. So nothing happened for
five or six weeks.

About three weeks ago, it appeared that the Executive
Board was going to make another selection, and I was
not impressed with any of the finalists, so I took
it upon myself to ask to meet with the Executive
Board, at which time I told them that I would not
vote for these persons and I was sure that if I didn't,
none would gain the 33 votes, the two-thirds majority
required. So, I said let's take a long hard look at
this. After all, we had stalled for a year-and-a-half.
So, they took another long look at it and decided
perhaps they should have advertised nationally for a
person to fill the job. I said, no, I thought there

were persons right in the State of Nebraska who could fill the job. This did not necessarily preclude people from outside the state. I received many, many calls at all hours of the day and night from people who felt that I was the person who could put the hand on their shoulder. I knew then that I could not name the Ombudsman, but I felt that I had enough support in the unicameral that I could block the appointment of one who did not fill the bill.

The Board decided to look around some more. We had a former Tax Commissioner who had been an army officer and was a very fine person, Mr. Murrell McNeil. I did not know him as well, but based upon the knowledge I had working with him during the few years he served in the Tax Commissioner's office, I felt that he would be a fine choice. I knew his sincerity in regard to performance would be excellent, and his knowledge of government is such that he can act effectively. I think he would do a good job.

They wanted to know if I would support him. I said I would. I tried to hurry it just a bit, so I could bring him with me here. Mechanically it just was not possible by a matter of a day or so, unfortunately, to get him here.

Just before I left yesterday, the Chairman of the
Executive Board told me that he has the unanimous
approval of the Executive Board and would be nominated.
He was nominated today, and I think he will have no
problem getting 33 votes.

Salary again is going to be a matter of controversy.
I think it needs to be somewhere around $22,000, which
is what McNeil received as Tax Commissioner. He has
retirement income, so salary is not that important to
him. I hope they do not adjust the salary so that it
is not on a level with top administrative officials
in state government.

The Ombudsman is going to have problems with the
Nebraska Legislature because some influential members
have opposed the bill, and I am afraid will not accept
the idea even now. There will be some persons who
will approve Mr. McNeil, I am sure, because he is a
former appointee of the Republican Governor and is
presently working for the Legislature as a research
person.

I am envious of Hawaii, because you did have a strong person who more or less led the way. I want to also thank the State of Hawaii for having had this legislation and for having appointed Mr. Doi, to whom I could point in seeking to reassure the apprehensive members of our legislature.

I agree that we can make mistakes in this program in years to come, but we can make very few mistakes at this time. I was determined that the first one had to be a good one. I would hope that legislators elsewhere have someone in mind for the job when they introduce their bills.

Ombudsman Walton:

I am sure you are familiar with the similarity between what is happening now and what happened with the city manager profession back in the thirties. I imagine there were conferences like this talking about the same thing. Historically, the first generation of managers came out of the community, and people were concerned that the managers be of sufficient stature to make it successful. The second and third generation have departed almost one hundred percent from the concept of selecting within the agency or within the area. Now they make a point of going outside the community. School

superindendants are another example. They want somebody who can bring in some new ideas. But how important it was initially that they were from within the
organization or community and that they had that
prestige! It will be interesting ten or fifteen years
from now to see if this same pattern holds for the
Ombudsman.

Professor Moore:
Well, Lee, I don't think we have to wait that long.
Seattle/King County skipped a generation--they moved
directly to a nationwide search. However, that
generation was not easily skipped, was it Liem?
Wasn't there considerable tension involved in making
the selection, and concern with finding a local
appointee?

Seattle/King County
Councilman Tuai:
Our bill provides that there shall be a Citizens'
Commission--three from the County and three from the
City, plus a chairman chosen by the six--who will go
through the screening process and give us the five
individuals who they feel are best qualified for the
job. The County and the City Council would then pick
from those five the individual who should be the joint
City-County Ombudsman.

This was in about January, 1971. They started advertising nationwide for the position, and we got some 200 applications, not only from the immediate area, but as far away as Panama, Puerto Rico, and all over the East Coast, the West Coast and in between. The Citizens' Commission asked the City and the County to allow their personnel officers to become involved in this, to help them go through the applications and to rate them as much as possible so that they would not have to go through the whole 200. They did. The personnel people were very good at it. They reduced the number down to about 35 that the Citizens' Commission should consider.

I'd just like to go back and give you some of the background on this Commission. There were six men and one woman: the woman is very active in civic affairs, the League of Women Voters type of thing, very knowledgeable, the wife of a political science professor at the University of Washington. There was a black who was involved in some of the community activities; a city manager type; a junior high school principal; a newspaper publisher; and two more I don't recall just off hand. It shows you the broad spectrum of people that were involved, and it turned

out that we were very fortunate in having this broad
spectrum.

These people, then, proceeded to go through the 35
candidates. They narrowed it down to 15 they wanted to
interview, including 6 from Washington and 9
from outside of the state. Now, we did not tell the
7 people who they were to pick, or give them any
specifications or criteria as to what they were to
look for, other than that this person had to be
extremely sensitive to the needs of a city which has a
black population of about 10%, an oriental population
of about 5% and some other noncaucasian population of
I'd say roughly 3 to 4%. The county, I would say, is
basically all white. There may be a percentage or two
of noncaucasian there.

I think they did an extremely good job of trying to
set forth to themselves what the criteria should be.
They examined the concept, they borrowed all the
materials that I had, and I think they all became
quite well educated as to what this person should be
like, prior to his selection. They took a month-and-
a-half to advertise, and then in February they started
interviewing. In three days of interviewing they

narrowed it down to five individuals. I sat through two days of the interviews. They then submitted these five names to the City and County Councils.

Thereafter, we set up a meeting with the five individuals, who basically were all involved in government. One had a law degree, but most of them were city manager types. The rest of the people just did not qualify as having any knowledge of how the government operated or who to talk to, who to see, how to get things done. So these five individuals were all interviewed on a Sunday. As most of you know, we chose Leland Walton. I think I can safely say that he was head and shoulders above the rest of the people that were involved. He was also chosen number one by the Citizens group. Now, I was the only one that knew that; the others did not know. Obviously, we feel that we got the best man that was available to us.

We have a Police Review Board already, and again it's hidden. It's not something that everybody knows of, and to this point it's never been used. It's the Human Rights Department of our city. It is criticizing the police quite often because of the number of blacks

and their aspirations, and, unfortunately, we have
had three shootings of blacks, two in the last
couple of months. The inquest jury was out on one,
and another was shot that morning. So it's a real
problem. The Human Rights Department has the right
to subpoena--for any records and individuals in the
city. It has never been employed. It was going
to do so with the Fire Department one time, but it
was talked out of it, I think by the Mayor.

So, I don't expect that the Ombudsman will be a
Police Review Committee, because right now I don't
think that if you asked the citizens of Seattle/King
County if they wanted a Police Review Board that you
would find very many people who are in favor of it.

We have an ongoing Committee composed of three members
from each of the two councils, and it will help set
the policies and the direction of the Ombudsman Office.
I might indicate that the old time Councilman who
was originally appointed to the Committee has been
replaced (because he's now become President of the
Council) by a former police officer who is on the
Council. I asked very purposely that he be put on
because I think with him on it he'll know what's going

on and he'll be less desirous of criticizing what's going to be done. I think we are going to neutralize the possible effect of his being on the outside looking in, to criticize.

Now, you can say that Leland will be a kept man, but I don't anticipate that. I have given him my pledge that he's going to run the office the way he wants to. He's going to seek guidance from us, and that's what we'll probably be there to help him with.

The County has a partisan government--five Republicans, four Democrats--which created a few problems in getting final approval of Leland's appointment. We had to wait about three weeks, because they couldn't get their ducks in line.

The City hasn't had these problems. I think we have our ducks in line. The City is committed to the program and I think that Leland will find no problems with us. But, in the County, as I indicated, politics are coming in. They have raised some questions about the budget now. They want to be sure that the number two man--well, actually there will be two deputies, one for the City and one for the County--they want

to be sure that these two individuals are paid
$17,000. Immediately, you say, why $17,000? Why is
it magical? Why should it be set at that? Our
advertising says $12,000 to $15,000. Well, unfortunately,
the present acting Ombudsman is making $17,000, and I
think the coincidence there is just so glaring,
that it's obvious. I personally have no feelings
whatsoever about the present acting Ombudsman, except
that he happened at one time to be campaign chairman
for one of the County councilmen who was fighting this
program. So I assume that if Leland was to appoint
him as the County Deputy that there would be no
problems. But, again, as I told Leland, this
is his prerogative this is his baby, he's going to
have to live through it and he's going to appoint
somebody that he can work with and who will help the
office. I would hope that we are not stuck with this
guy if he's not a suitable enough person.

Again, on the City side, we have a man appointed
by the Mayor who's in charge of the Citizens Service
Bureau. So far as I'm concerned there is no pressure
at all from the City for the appointment of that
individual, as the Deputy from the City. And all
this leads me to say that I believe very strongly in a

non-partisan City Council because the way it's set
up we can get things done, we don't have this
partisan politics problem. The County has it every day.

I think I'll just close by indicating that, as far as
the City Council was concerned with the appointment
of the individual, I went around and talked to all of
the Council people and said that three of us would be
out looking at this person, and if we come up with
a person, would they agree? And it was unanimous that
the other six would go with whomever we three chose.
So, we were very fortunate in arriving at that stage
of the game where the rest of the Council would agree
on the man that we chose. In the County Council,
several of the people who agreed to such a setup backed
away at the last minute, and that's why we didn't
have enough votes for a couple of weeks.

We are very parochial right now. Because Boeing is
laying off so many people, we feel that we should
hire local people, and it seems that we have been
going outside the state in hiring most of the upper
echelon of people for our government. The fact that
we had the Citizens' Commission go through this
selection gave us an out. We could say that "very

47

interested and informed citizens gave us these five
people and the Ordinance provides that we are to
pick from these five, and since all five are from
outside of the state, we had no choice." It has, I think,
cooled off most of the criticism that would have come
if we in the City and the County had formed our own
committee and started going through a group of people,
because then I think they'd still be after us for the
fact that we went outside the state when there are
so many people theoretically qualified within the
area.

Ombudsman Walton:
Since I am from out of state, I think to a great extent
this is an advantage, and I made that point to the
reporters. However, to compensate for this fact, I
certainly make no secret of the fact that the two
chief deputies--to compensate perhaps for my lack of
familiarity with the local problems and with the
local situation--would be local. Hopefully, too,
I would like to have at least one on the staff with a
legal background.

Professor Moore:
I note in your closing remarks the possibility that
these deputies might be selected from the existing
pseudo-ombudsmanic offices for the City and the County,

which in turn suggests a possibility that they may be thinking of phasing those operations out, or of incorporating them within the Ombudsman office.

Councilman Tuai:
From the City standpoint, the person now involved in the Citizens' Service Bureau handles all kinds of phone calls and I think he probably does a pretty good job. He also runs the tours of the City Hall. I think the Mayor will probably keep him on for that public relations purpose of taking care of the school kids and telling people where to go if they want to get a building permit, this type of thing, rather than to answer complaints. I hope that the Mayor will cooperate with this; he may not, I don't know. I would hope so, though.

Ombudsman Walton:
I'm just going to make one comment before we leave, in terms of my own acceptance of the appointment. I certainly had some trepidations. My interest came about as a result of having read and talked with a couple of people, and this was sort of a dream come true, in the sense that I've been involved with public administration most of my adult life and although I've suffered a great many frustrations, here it seemed as though·finally at last, there was an

opportunity to participate in something unique.
I think that was what really intrigued me--the
uniqueness of this in terms of experiment in local
government. But I had some strong reservations in
my own mind about being exclusively engaged in
responding to complaints. I doubted that after the
initial period of establishment and developing procedures and so forth, that this in itself would be
adequate. What certainly turned my decision in
favor of the position has to do with the Ombudsman's
other powers, "to undertake, to participate, and to
cooperate with general studies or enquiries, whether
or not related to any particular administrative
agency or any particular administrative act, if he
believes that that may enhance knowledge about and
lead to improvements in the functioning of
administrative agencies."

Among all the responsibilities that the office entails,
I think this is the one that I felt was the icing on
the cake. In other words, I suspect for a couple of
years I'll have all I can handle in terms of
organizing, establishing, getting the things running,
hopefully establishing some credibility for the
office in general. But ultimately, over a period of

years, I think that clause contains the real opportunity of this job to make additional contributions. I
don't know exactly what I have in mind yet. I'm not
entirely clear how that can be used, but at least
they have seen fit to encompass within the scope of
the powers of the office this kind of ability to deal
with other than specific complaints about specific
acts. This ability to deal with broad problems,
not initially but ultimately, will be the real meat
of the office.

SUMMARY

Professor Anderson:
In a way, I think it's the unique quality of the
Ombudsman office that it serves as the buckle between
the particular and the general. It is from the
particular problems that you are able to propose
improvements.

I have just a quick concluding comment. It draws
on all three of the presentations. It seems that there
are two basic ways to find a good Ombudsman. One,
you know the man beforehand. That is, everyone
looks at him and says, "There's an Ombudsman!"
Well, in that case the machinery doesn't really matter.
You should go through the formalities as a matter of
due process, but the machinery isn't too important.

The other situation is where you don't have such a man. That is where the machinery, such as they had in Seattle, is extremely important. Here, the nominating group should not be composed of members of the appointing body.

Senator Schmit:

Looking back, the least we could have done would have been to provide for nominations from the floor of the Legislature in the event the Board decided to just stall for time.

Senator Kawasaki:

I just want to make one point. In my judgment, the retention of the appellation Ombudsman is really important. This arouses curiosity among the public
sector. They want to know what this office/about. They begin to read whenever there is an article in the newspaper about the Ombudsman. As a matter of fact, the morning paper ran a sort of a contest for someone to suggest a new name. A number of Hawaiian names were suggested, but all were rejected. This arouses public curiosity, and they begin to identify the duties of that office with the particular name Ombudsman.

Professor Moore:
Loran, I just wondered if in practice you were using
the term Ombudsman, even though the formal designation
is Public Counsel?

Senator Schmit:
The public and the press and the Legislature refer to
it as the Ombudsman.

Ombudsman Walton:
I think this is important in terms of stature. When you
use the term Ombudsman, the ears perk up and it has a
sort of immediate credibility or respectability.

Councilman Tuai:
Of course, ours is not formally designated Ombudsman.
It is called the Joint Seattle/King County Office of
Citizens Complaints.

Senator Kawasaki:
How long is the tenure of your Ombudsman?

Ombudsman Walton:
Five years, and this is something I want to bring
up this afternoon. I would be interested in hearing
your comments on whether or not he should be subject
to reappointment.

Councilman Tuai:
Don't let that mislead you, Leland, you will also find
in there a provision that if the money is cut off...

That's a good point. It takes a two-thirds majority
to remove him, but it only takes a majority to
remove the appropriation.

HAWAII'S OMBUDSMAN: THE CONTEXT OF
RELATED GRIEVANCE MECHANISMS

Professor Moore:

As Senator Kawasaki made clear this morning, Hawaii
had in Herman Doi, an exceptionally well-qualified
candidate for the position of Ombudsman. It also
afforded an exceptionally conducive setting for the
success of the Ombudsman office. If you look at the
array of complementary mechanisms to be found in Hawaii,
you would be able to identify several that could be
located in almost any state; it is the combination of
so many complementary mechanisms that has made the
setting so advantageous.

There are, to begin with, the internal grievance
mechanisms located within the agencies themselves.
These are most fully developed in the Departments of
Social Services, Labor and Industrial Relations, Health,
and in the Honolulu Police Department.

Related to these internal appeals procedures are the
vigorous public employee organizations that provide

54

representation and assistance for public employees
who wish to pursue grievances with their employer.
There is a Legal Aid Society that is really a com-
posite of a number of formerly separate legal aid
activities. There is a Commission on Judicial
Qualifications, which is patterned after the California
prototype. It has the potential to pursue complaints
directed at members of the judiciary, but as the
present Chief Justice views the Commission, he sees
a much more limited function; one that is concerned
almost exclusively with the physical and mental
vitality of judges. There is, however, a possibility of
its assuming a broader role here. There is an Office
of Consumer Protection that is quite vigorous and has
an extensive staff and some strong legislation to
support it. It was established as a semiautonomous
agency at the same time that the Ombudsman office
began in July, 1969. There is a State Ethics Commission
that is empowered to pursue, either on its motion or
in response to complaints, questions regarding conflict
of interest and so forth. There is an Office of
Legislative Auditor that had displayed considerable
vigor. In fact, on an almost annual basis he has
gone through each of the departments and prepared what
amounts to a white paper, and in some cases he has

wrung them out and hung them up to dry. An Ombudsman would be reluctant to proceed, I think, with quite the same aggressive attitude.

Ombudsman Walton:
There should be an interchange of information between the two offices.

Ombudsman Doi:
There is. The person who is in charge of the Auditor's office used to work with me in the Legislative Reference Bureau.

Professor Moore:
It is very important that you have that kind of relationship with the Legislative Auditor, because otherwise there is a grey area in which the two jurisdictions could overlap. Proceeding with our catalog of complementary mechanisms, legislative casework continues while, as Senator Kawasaki indicated, the Ombudsman office affords an opportunity to legislators to get rid of the birddogging that they don't want to do. They retain the option of pursuing those complaints that they think it would be useful to pursue.

The City and County of Honolulu, which contains 80% of the population of the islands, has an Office of

Information and Complaint that handles a very large
volume of complaints and inquiries in a manner different
from the Ombudsman office, but complementary to it.
For the most part, complaints are disposed of very
rapidly, using the telephone and going from the Office
of Information and Complaint to the lowest level in
the agency at which action might be taken, where the
general practice of the Ombudsman office is to proceed
through the higher levels of the agency. The Office of
Information and Complaint is presently handling something like 11,000 inquiries per year.

There are newspaper action lines which have the
potential of providing a complementary service, and
in Honolulu I think they realize that potential.
They are not "Dear Abby" columns. They respond to
substantive complaints about governmental services,
and the people who run these action lines are looking
for complaints that might be generalizable, so that
in responding to one complaint in the newspaper they
may forestall a series of complaints on the same
subject. Scoops Casey--the action line lady who calls
herself "Miss Fixit"--estimates that she receives
between 30 and 50 inquiries a day. She responds to
about five of those in her column, and answers the

others either by telephone or letter. When I com-
plimented her on the kind of screening that she does,
and on the substance of her column, she commented
that she had just been chided by her editor as he
relayed two complaints that the column was too heavy.
The letters called for something a little jazzier, and
one of them included a copy of the column from an
Albuquerque newspaper that was more in that style.
This suggests a tension that may exist in a newspaper
column between a desire to increase circulation and a
desire to perform some kind of public service.
Nevertheless, I think the action line columns are
exceptionally good in Hawaii, and do perform a
meaningful complaint-handling function.

Legislation has now been adopted to establish an
Office of Information in the Governor's office that
would perform at the state level something like the
service provided by the Honolulu Office of Information and Complaint. There is also an Ombudsman for
the University of Hawaii, although the State Ombudsman
has statutory jurisdiction over the University. Here,
I think the complementary relationship is clear.

As you scan this array of complementary mechanisms,

I think it is notable that some of them preceded the Ombudsman office, some got underway simultaneously with the Ombudsman office, and some of them have emerged subsequent to and as a result of the Ombudsman office. It was partly in response to Herman Doi's recommendation that the Governor sought legislation to establish a State Office of Information.

The prison system now has an internal grievance mechanism that it didn't have until Herman Doi began to receive complaints from the prisoners, and then from their guards, and finally from prison officials who weren't too happy about his intervention in behalf of the first two groups. He suggested to them that if they were to take the initiative, he wouldn't have to tread on their turf quite so much. So they initiated their own grievance procedures.

This brief survey provides you with a very rough idea of what the context is like. We'll have an opportunity to go into the nature of these related services to-morrow. Herman can, I am sure, help us to better understand how he went about assuring that these complementary services would be converted into sources of support for his office rather than sources of competition.

Ombudsman Doi:
Let me amplify on the complementary services. There
are some that John did not mention. Perhaps they have
not been operational before. We have on Maui a Board
of Appeals which is provided for by their Charter,
which is supposed to be like an Ombudsman for their
County. As I understand it, they have had only one
complaint go to the Board of Appeals so far. In the
Counties of Maui and Kauai, the Administrative
Assistants to the Mayor are fielding complaints from
members of the public. Those are extra sources of
information and also relief for members of the public.

For example, I serve on the Media Council with the T.V.
station managers and the newspaper editors.

Professor Moore:
Was that just recently established? I remember reading
an editorial that favored it.

Ombudsman Doi:
They receive complaints about the media, about newspaper coverage. It's a group of citizens, plus the
press who sit on this Media Council and we are still
in the process of trying to work out some systematic
way of being effective. You have to get involved with

these various groups that are performing related
functions, like the Media Council.

During the last session, the Governor was authorized
to set up an Office of Information. Now, what he will
do with that, of course, is as yet unknown. They may
well handle the complaints that come to them by
referring such complaints to the agencies, which to my
way of thinking is all right. As we go through our
own procedures, you'll see that initially we would
like the citizen to go to the department and try
to see whether he cannot resolve his problem by
himself. Secondly, and more importantly, it gives
the administrator in charge of the program the first
opportunity to settle the problem at that level, rather
than having to appeal to a higher level.

Ombudsman Walton:
How did you make this known to the public at large?

Ombudsman Doi:
As the individual comes to us, we very deliberately
ask him whether or not he has contacted the department
at all. If he has not, we suggest that he do so.

Ombudsman Walton:
Do you get any resentment for that reaction?

Ombudsman Doi:

Not necessarily. We'll tell him specifically who
he can call to try to have his problem resolved, with
the invitation that if he cannot, please come back
to us.

Mr. Kaye:

Herman, do you check to see whether that particular
department or agency has publicly made known its own
internal mechanism?

Ombudsman Doi:

In many instances, the complainants don't know.what
mechanism is appropriate. If it's a workmens'
compensation problem we are familiar with the
operations of the Department, so we know whom to refer
him to, and we'll tell him, and give him the specific
name of the person and the telephone number that he
should contact. In some cases we may even go so far
as to contact the person and tell him that "This
person came to us, we gave him your name and address
and phone number and he'll get in touch with you.
Please try to see whether you can resolve the problem
in your own way." If they cannot, then the
complainant is always free to come back to us and
we'll take a good look at it. We think the agency
should have the first crack at it.

In getting this assignment of what steps to go through in setting up an Office of the Ombudsman, I was faced with a kind of dilemma, because the easiest choice would have been to go through the regular sequence of events that you have to go through, like having to find office space and a secretary and all the rest of it. But, I think that kind of problem is too elementary and everyone will consider such problems. So, what I tried to do was outline the various kinds of decisions that possibly you would be faced with.

The first thing that we mentioned is, of course, to do the necessary reading in the subject area, which I'm sure whoever is appointed as an Ombudsman will do automatically. In that respect, there is a wealth of information as far as the theory of ombudsmanship and what some of the objectives of the office are. As you go through the various readings, you'll see that many different authors will repeat the kinds of objectives that an Ombudsman should have. In doing your reading, I think your list will grow.

The other things you ought to look at are the reports

of Ombudsmen from other jurisdictions. I think they
will give you some idea of the kinds of cases that are
handled, and the kinds of cases that are handled
jurisdiction by various jurisdictions do not differ
that much, really. The application of the laws,
rules and regulations may be different, but not the
kinds of basic problems that we face.

Determining Objectives

Ombudsman Doi:

I think it is important that the office identify some
of the objectives that it wants to attain. In determining your objectives you will be automatically
determining where you will be going with the office,
and it lends the kind of tone to the office that is
necessary. The objectives that we have identified
for outselves are seven in number:

(1) Redress of individual grievances;

(2) Prevent recurrence of similar complaints;

(3) Increase responsiveness of administrators;

(4) Protect government administrators from unfounded
     criticism;

(5) Identify and correct patterns of undesirable
     administrative practices or procedures;

(6) Education of the public about governmental operations
     and functions; and

(7) Relieve legislators of the complaint-handling
     burden.

The seven seem to run in a descending order of priority. However, let's start from the bottom-- relieving legislators of complaint-handling burdens. We have not had as many complaints referred from legislators as we have had individual persons coming to us directly. It is noticeable that we have been getting referrals from legislators of both the majority and minority parties, so to me that is heartening.

The education function is something that you are going to have to do. That is, in the process of handling complaints, you are going to have to tell the complainant what he could have done for himself, what functions of government are being performed by various agencies, and what their limitations of power are. So I think you play an educational role also.

Of course, it is also important to realize that we are here to protect government administrators from unfounded criticism. This is part of the objective role that the Ombudsman must play. Increased responsiveness of administrators is something that is immeasurable, but we have heard comments from administrators that

since our office was established they are much more
careful in how their people respond to citizens
who are complaining about their services, because
they know they may come to us, and then have to go
through a long series of explanations in proving
their point of view and their decision.

The recurrence of similar complaints provides a
hint of possible procedural problems and it is
important that we check to see that the same
types of problems do not reoccur.

The main purpose for the existence of the Ombudsman's
office is to redress individual grievances that are
justified.

Jurisdictional Limitations
Ombudsman Doi:
I think you play an educational role in another
sense, and that is in defining what an Ombudsman may
do. You will have to explain the exclusions that are
made from the jurisdiction of the Ombudsman.
Many people ask why the Legislature is excluded,
why our legislators, the governor, and the courts
are excluded, why federal agencies are excluded, why
multi-state agencies are excluded. So, in
explanation, you will have to talk about representative

democratic government, in the sense that these
are elected officials, they are elected for a term of
office, and the people are really the repository of power
who pass judgment on their abilities periodically at
elections. I think that is the basic reason for the
exclusion.

The courts are much harder to put on that basis. The
argument that we have come up with is that the court
is supposed to be the final forum for the settling
of disputes between individuals and between an
individual and his government, and there has to be
some finality.

Federal agencies are excluded because the State does
not have jurisdiction over a national governmental
agency. Multistate agencies are formed by compacts
between states and thus no individual state has
jurisdiction over such an entity.

If I were to compare the Hawaii statute against most
other jurisdictions, I think we have about the minimum
number of exclusions from our jurisdiction as compared
to other jurisdictions. Let me give you an example
of that. In Great Britain, after the receipt of the

complaint, it takes several days before they make up their minds whether or not they have jurisdiction. There are many specific exclusions from jurisdiction, so they have to run down a whole list of things to see whether or not it falls within one of the exclusions. Now this is spending time in order to determine that you do not have jurisdiction, which I really think is a waste of time. Since we have a minimum number of exclusions we make this kind of decision rather quickly. In fact, a staff member makes it.

Mr. Douglas:
You do not take complaints about federal agencies?

Ombudsman Doi:
We cannot investigate a case involving a federal agency, but what we have done in some cases is just make the referral to the appropriate person who they can contact to get some relief. In some cases, we have gone ahead and gotten the information as to what the person had to do. This applies especially to the no-jurisdiction area. For example, we have had complaints about the legislators. We try to tell
the complainants/they may do in order to relieve some
        what
of their frustrations. We had a complaint once from a person who was in a veterans hospital in Virginia,

68

which I sent to our senators and congressmen from Hawaii, and they got after the Veterans Administration. What happened to the person, I do not know.

Mr. Douglas:
I have done a lot of complaint handling in the Mayor's office, and that's the way we operate. We have no real jurisdiction over anybody except the City departments. The majority of our complaints are against county welfare and things like that. We really operate it by persuasion.

Ombudsman Doi:
For example, we have contacted the local social security agency. They have given us information about the case and told us to have the person call them, and they'd be more than happy to speak with him. This is on a very informal basis, since we had no jurisdiction whatsoever.

Professor Moore:
I gather, Herman, that it is largely a question of allocating scarce resources--if you have the staff available and the time to pursue complaints that fall outside your jurisdiction.

Housekeeping

Professor Anderson:
We are thinking here of guidance for someone who is about to open an Ombudsman Office. You have a lot of

things going at the same time--record-keeping decisions, staffing decisions and so on. I know it is a juggling act. So, how did you juggle it, and how would you recommend that somebody else do it when they are first trying to get off the ground?

Ombudsman Doi:
My thought when I first started was that I wanted to know every blasted thing that I could possibly learn about handling a complaint by myself before hiring the first staff member. I wanted to have that experience under my belt in order to be able to tell other people how to handle complaints. So, I started with myself and one secretary for about three months, and did everything by myself, until it got to be rather unbearable, and then I hired the first lawyer.

Professor Anderson:
Did you hold back on publicity at that point so as not to be overwhelmed by the sheer numbers of complaints?

Ombudsman Doi:
No, we had a tremendous amount of publicity, and we got a tremendous number of complaints.

Ombudsman Walton:
If you were doing it again, would you staff up initially to handle them?

Ombudsman Doi:
No, I would do it myself.

Professor Anderson:
How much time did you have just in terms of getting
space, a desk, a telephone, before you started?
Did you have at least a minimal physical plant?

Ombudsman Doi:
Yes, I had made these arrangements even before I
took office, by having space allocated to me by
the appropriate department. Then, I hired my
secretary even before we started. That was easy,
because she worked with me at the Legislative Reference Bureau and had already been working in the
State Legislature, so she was no longer in civil
service. So she came with me. Only July 1, both of
us appeared at the office and we had desks already
sent in--we borrowed desks from the Legislature--in
order to start our office.

Mr. Douglas:
Did you ever return them?

Ombudsman Doi:
Yes, we bought all our own equipment thereafter.

Publicity

Ombudsman Doi:
I think there are basically two types of information
dissemination that you have to be concerned about. The
first involves educating the public as to the existence

of the office, and what the office can and may do.
Now, we have not been very successful in this respect.
I think the number of no jurisdiction cases that we are
still getting is probably at approximately the same
level as during the first year, which indicates to
me that there is some confusion in the mind of the
public as to what we can handle and what we cannot
handle.

The second kind of information dissemination I think
that you are going to run across involves deciding
how you are going to operate your office. There are
basically two ways. One can be that you are going
to be a publicity hound: every case that you
settle is going to be advertised and publicized.
This makes the office look good--the Ombudsman is
really doing things. I think the shortcoming of
that method is that administrators are not going
to cooperate with you. If you don't know it by now,
administrators can make it awfully difficult for
you to get information by many subtleties. They may
give you only a portion of the information that is
required to make the decision, in which case you
have to pick out the rest by physically going through
their file, and that is going to take time. There

are also the kinds of subtleties that I think everybody who has been in public administration recognizes.
They can start playing games with you by throwing up
straw men and all the rest of it. So in deciding what
kind of office you want to run, I think you have to
take into consideration the fact that it is important
to develop a pretty good relationship with the administrators. Now, the course that Hawaii chose was for the
office to operate on a fairly quiet level. We have
never made a public release on any case thus far.
We have never used publicity as a weapon as yet.

Councilman Tuai:
Do the reporters get on your back at all?

Ombudsman Doi:
They come around every once and a while, and we may
discuss cases very informally with them, without
mentioning names. But we have had the situation
turned around on us; that is, we have had complainants
who have had their complaints disposed of go to the
press. We have had a few of those cases.

Ombudsman Walton:
How do you respond to a press inquiry about a fellow
who thinks he got a bad deal from you?

Ombudsman Doi:
There we ask the person to get in touch with us and

allow us to release whatever information we have in the files. Each complaint is still considered confidential. In most cases, the complainants will not give the press their consent.

Professor Anderson:
Herman, to what extent does that policy of concern for rapport with administrators feed into the preparation of your annual report? In other words, would you say there is nothing in here that might give a few grey hairs to an administrator?

Ombudsman Doi:
I am sure that the report contains information that will give grey hairs to some administrators, although they have not responded in that fashion yet.

Professor Anderson:
In some Ombudsman jurisdictions they have a problem of cyclical publicity. When they turn out their annual report, the press picks it up. Thereafter, it tails off for the rest of the year. But you haven't had that?

Ombudsman Doi:
I haven't had that. We have had no problems with the press as yet. We have been quite open with the press.

Ombudsman Walton:
They don't harass you, in the sense of trying to get

specific stories out of you?

Ombudsman Doi:
They have on occasion, yes.

The problem that we have run across by operating at a low level, I think, is a problem that you may well run across, and that is that not very many people are going to know about what you have accomplished. So, pretty soon they may start asking what do we have an Ombudsman for? Maybe the questions have started in Hawaii. So we are thinking of different ways of handling this problem.

This is one of the problems we are going to have to solve. That is, how can we provide coverage for accomplishments of the Ombudsman, and at the same time maintain good relations with the administrators and the public.

Professor Anderson:
Herman, do top administrators and the legislators know what you are doing, pretty much? Doesn't one administrator know that you've had maybe a pretty tough case with another one? Is there a kind of grapevine?

Ombudsman Doi:

I'm sure there is a grapevine operating among the administrators themselves. But I'm not sure whether the grapevine extends to the press.

Professor Anderson:

Does it extend to the Legislature?

Ombudsman Doi:

I'm pretty sure they know what's happening in state government. One of the readings that you can get is the feedback from legislators themselves. We have had no adverse comments on the part of the legislators themselves yet, but it may still be the honeymoon period.

Ombudsman Walton:

How about the news media? Have you started to get any feedback from them?

Ombudsman Doi:

As far as adverse publicity goes, we have had one editorial comment about the cost per case, and the fact that we are increasing our request for appropriations. When they appropriated the funds to our office this year there was some comment by the editor of one newspaper that the cost per case was around $100. He took the total number of inquiries for the first year and divided it by total appropriations, and it came out to $100 per case.

Professor Moore:

Herman, wasn't that in part precipitated by the
annoyance of that particular editorial staff with the
proposal for the creation of an Office of Information
in the Governor's office? They linked the two, and
pointed out that your office had recommended that this
additional mechanism be instituted.

Ombudsman Doi:

I am not sure what the motivation is. I have invited
the head of the newspaper to come down and look at our
operation in case he had any doubts about it.

Professor Anderson:

It is a no-win situation in trying to tell the public
about your successes, for the simple reason that you're
trying to make people feel that government is basically
honest, efficient, responsive, and so on, and you are
going to work against that if you go out and say,
"look I straightened out the department of this-or-that."
The department, of course, would go wild.

Perhaps you could meet both of your objectives here
just by publicizing the percentages of justified and
unjustified complaints: you would be protecting government administrators, by pointing out that a substantial
percentage of the administrators are upheld, and
you would be convincing the average citizen that he

could get a hearing because a substantial percentage of the complaints appear to be justified. That is a very generalized approach that might not meet some of the problems of revealing individual cases.

Ombudsman Doi:
Well, I was thinking about finding some in-between way of handling the situation. I have not come up with any solution as yet. I know it's going to be a problem as we go along.

Ombudsman Walton:
Have you had any celebrated kind of case that couldn't avoid the spotlight, for example, where a policeman shot a kid or something?

Ombudsman Doi:
No, we haven't had that kind of case. We did make a press release at the time that we found that the public utilities had to pay interest on their deposits. The complainant went to the newspaper himself and told the newspaper the Ombudsman did this for us and then we had the press all over us finding out what was happening.

We have had inquiries on some of the cases from the newspaper after they found out that we had received complaints about the case. Our position has always

been that we will not release any information until the
case is concluded. By that time, a newsworthy story
is gone. In the course of the investigation we have
not released news about the case.

You will notice that where there is a lot of
publicity about a case, administrators are going to
respond much sooner because they know it is a hot case.
They are going to respond to the Ombudsman fairly
fast. They are not going to stall around; it is
not to their benefit to do so.

Professor Wyner:
Herman, have you ever gone on the luncheon circuit?

Ombudsman Doi:
Oh boy! You'll find a list of them in the annual
report.

Professor Wyner:
Is that at all an adequate way of publicizing the
office?

Ombudsman Doi:
It's one way. I've gone before HCAP (Hawaii Community
Action Program) groups in different communities, PTA's,
prison guards. I went to several training sessions
for new police cadets. I've been in one class in a
community college and one high school so far. I think

that is going to expand as time goes on. We have contacted the social studies curriculum specialist in
the school system, and I think that as part of the
information that is to be given to students there will
be mention of the fact that there is an Ombudsman
and what he does. In fact, we have had kids come in
for copies of our reports because they are doing research
papers on it, and all this kind of thing.

Ombudsman Walton:
I had a call from a Seattle radio station, or
rather a group of stations who called to say that they
would like to give me a half-hour a week for Ombudsman
publicity. I said that I would like to talk it over
with my committee in Seattle, but the more I thought
about it, the more pitfalls I saw in that kind of
approach. You are going to risk the wrath of the
other media, and even if you try to discuss cases on
an anonymous basis, it's likely to reflect adversely
on the administrative department.

Professor Anderson:
It is a dilemma, because you have to have enough time
to explain to people with some particularity what you
are doing, in order for them to have a proper
understanding. I think the little brochure that
Herman has developed is a very good idea, because you

do have enough space to tell them in some modest
detail just what you are doing. (See Appendix II.)

Ombudsman Walton:
How do you get the booklet out? Is there a general
mailing?

Ombudsman Doi:
No, but we furnish HCAP and legal aid with hundreds
of these brochures, so they can pass it round, to be
sure we are reaching low income areas.

Professor Anderson:
What would you think, Herman, of a movie of your
operation--15-25 minutes for use in schools or
service clubs? Do you think that would be a helpful way to publicize it? Perhaps it would take a
little bit of the pressure off the personal appearances.

Ombudsman Doi:
I doubt that you are going to get away from personal
appearances. We are working on a slide show now,
which we can use in conjunction with making speeches.

Ombudsman Walton:
Of course, if there ever comes a time when there are
enough Ombudsmen, a person might be able to put together
an all-purpose movie collage dealing with the subject
for general distribution. You probably can't substitute for personal appearances, though.

Professor Anderson:
How long did you wait before you started accepting
invitations to speak to service groups and other
public meetings?

Ombudsman Doi:
Initially, by confining myself to night meetings, I was
able to devote my time to handling complaints during
the day and speaking at night.

Councilman Tuai:
About how many inquiries per week or per month do you
get from the Press?

Ombudsman Doi:
Not very many. I would say in the last six months
I had about four phone calls from T.V. stations or from
newspaper reporters about the cases, and I have told
them I can't discuss the case with them.

Ombudsman Walton:
Do they give you pretty good coverage? Do they
print your press releases or do they carry informational
stories on occasion?

Ombudsman Doi:
We have received invitations from "Miss Fixit" that
anytime we want to publicize any information, she
would be more than willing to print it in her
column.

Professor Anderson:
Do you subscribe to a clipping service? Do you

try to get complete files on all newspaper items

relating to your own office?

Ombudsman Doi:
Yes, we do.

Professor Anderson:
How do you accomplish that?

Ombudsman Doi:
My secretary does that.

Professor Anderson:
You get all papers yourself from Hawaii?

Ombudsman Doi:
Yes.

Professor Anderson:
Weeklies?

Ombudsman Doi:
Not in the office. We have the morning papers come

in. She clips when she sees it in the evening paper,

or I clip when I see it; so we have a pretty complete

file.

Staff Appointments and Assignments

Ombudsman Doi:
What kind of staff should we get? Should it be a

low level staff in the sense of hiring investigators,

or should I hire professional people, or where

should I go on this problem? The first person I

hired was an attorney, and I'd made my decision about his professional training before he was hired. However, I went to Scandinavia to have a look at the various kinds of staffing ratios and staffing patterns, and the kinds of people that they hire.

There are noticeable differences between the Scandinavian countries and Great Britain. Great Britain hires nothing but civil servants. They work for three years in the Parliamentary Commissioner's office, and then they go back to civil service. He has not hired lawyers. To the Scandinavians this is unbelievable, because the Scandinavian countries hire nothing but jurists.

When I made up my mind as to the kind of personnel that I wanted, I sought a pretty high level staff that could develop an expertise that would be very difficult for the departments themselves to controvert. In other words, I felt that I needed a staff that was so competent that we could take the department on practically anything and be able to get at the facts and the law and the rules and regulations, so that by the time we got to an informal conference there was no doubt as to who was going to win. For that reason, I chose a small well qualified staff.

The kinds of people that I have hired so far include
a deputy who is also a lawyer and has had extensive
experience in state and local government. He was a
private attorney for a long period of time. He served
as a lobbyist for the city and County of Honolulu
at one time and also worked in our State Legislature.
I have another attorney who also has a Masters in
public administration and worked as an administrative
intern for the FAA and for state government.

We are experimenting with people other than attorneys,
by hiring a person with a Masters in guidance from
Columbia University who has served as a school
counsellor for many years. And the fourth person that
I have on my staff is a person who has a Masters in
political science and who had gone to school in Los
Angeles for a long period of time but who had come
to Hawaii and got his Masters here and had worked in
state government in Hawaii.

Professor Anderson:
Could I comment on this? One factor I think that enters
in here is the nature of the educational system that
trains the people that are looking for government
jobs in general.

In Scandinavia, the tradition is that a law
education is a general education, and many, many
students go to the law faculty. Only a few of them
then go on to become apprentices in law offices and
actually practice law. So that the whole civil
service is really made up of jurists, as they would
call them.

Whereas in England, they have a much more restrictive
tradition and a narrow specialization of the bar.
I guess we are somewhere in-between, and I think your
staffing reflects that in-between position.

Ombudsman Doi:
Well, I've deliberately hired persons other than
lawyers, because I wanted to see how well they would
do in a setting like this. And, I think they are
working out pretty well. The only thing that I
notice with the   nonlawyers, is that it takes a little
more time for them to do the legal research. You
have to do more training in legal research than you do
with a lawyer. They can overcome that disability in
no time. All you need is the bright young man who
is interested in researching and he can do it. Which
gets to my next point, that various disciplines will
serve equally well in an Ombudsman's office.

Ombudsman Walton:

In making assignments, do you attempt to assign to
the lawyer those cases which involve more expertise
in law, as opposed to the other disciplines, or do
you assign them in rotation?

Ombudsman Doi:

Rotation. In some complex or difficult cases where
it is noticeably a legal question, we may assign it
to one of the lawyers.

Ombudsman Walton:

But you do not attempt to develop particular areas
of specialty upon your staff. They are all generalists?

Ombudsman Doi:

That's another choice that I had to make, whether to
specialize in different areas. The shortcoming that
I saw in specialization in other jurisdictions, is that
once the specialist leaves you are stuck. And,
you are going to be stuck for a long time until you
develop somebody in that specialty. The other thing
I think you have to consider is that one person
working in the welfare area is going to get awfully
sick and tired of looking at welfare cases. Or, for
that matter, in education and so on. The fact that
they are handling all kinds of complaints keeps their
interest up and offers a new challenge for the staff.

I think that you will need somebody with legal
training on your staff. That is, many problems can be
resolved, or are resolved as a consequence of good
legal research, in the sense that you are limited by
what the law says, or you are limited by whatever rules
and regulations are in force which are in conformity
with law, so many of the problems are legal in nature.
In being a reasonable person, I think you have to
understand what the law says and what the limitations
of the departments are and how far they can act, and
what they can do and what they can't do.

Record-Keeping

What about record keeping? The forms that we use
are attached. (See Appendix I.) Record keeping is a
very onerous, a very time consuming chore. Again, I
think the identification of what you want your office
to be will determine the kinds of records that you
are going to have to keep. That's the reason why
it is important to try and pin down initially what
objectives you are seeking to have your office perform.
Then, you can relate your records to the kinds of
objectives that you have.

If you go to the reports, you'll find that practically
every Ombudsman reports on the number of cases that he

has, the number of cases that he has rectified, the number that he has found to be unjustified, and so forth.
Well, I think the crux of the matter is that the
reporting procedures that are employed by the
Ombudsmen in the various jurisdictions are not
comparable, in the sense that we don't know what we
are comparing. In our case, we have tried to break
down the number of inquiries we have had into three
different classifications. I'm not sure when I'm
comparing our complaint statistics against, say,
the Alberta statistics, if they involve only complaints,
or whether they involve inquiries of other kinds--
informational inquiries or no-jurisdiction inquiries.
So, it's very difficult to compare statistics.

If I had to start over again I think I would have
done a lot of thinking about record keeping way ahead
of time, and perhaps gone to some automated data keeping
system, rather than doing it manually as we are
doing now. We are in the process of automating our data.
In fact, I am working on a program with the University
Of Hawaii to see whether I can get the kind of information I want by use of their computers. We would
have to list the information we wanted and then
supply them with the necessary data. They would key

punch it and run it through the computer, so that it comes back in any shape and form that we want.

An important point is the confidentiality of each complaint. So, we will not be listing names. We'll be listing case numbers, and we will have them listed under various categories. There will be no way that the person who did the data processing will be able to identify the person who made the complaint.

Quebec has a system that is computer processable. They fill out the form, it's not an IBM card, it's a larger piece of paper which they run through a reader. Then this is transferred to the computer system.

Professor Anderson:
Did you refine your record keeping techniques as you went along, to tailor them to your experience? I wonder if that isn't always going to be the case-- if it wouldn't be too utopian to think that you could prepare the ultimate record-keeping system before you started. Obviously you should make the effort, but it seems to me that every jurisdiction is going to be different enough that you are going to be adjusting it as you go along, especially at the beginning.

Professor Moore:

But I think you can visualize a kind of modular system where you would have certain components that would be included in virtually every jurisdiction, and others that would be adjusted to particular circumstances.

Ombudsman Doi:

One of the things you have to consider is that you have to be flexible in your record-keeping system. Six months after we were in operation I met with my one other staff member and my secretary. We went over the record-keeping procedures to see whether we could improve it. After one year, we again went over our record keeping system and we have changed the record system quite a bit.

Ombudsman Walton:

Is there information which you wish you had started gathering in the initial phases, which is perhaps lost, specific types of information?

Ombudsman Doi:

We had that experience, I think, after six months. I was appointed in July 1, 1969, and the Legislature came into session on January 1, 1970, so I gave them a six months report. But in writing the report we found gaps in our record keeping system, so we had to go back through each case for the preceding six months and extract the information we needed.

Measuring Effectiveness

Ombudsman Doi:

I think the statistics have to be compiled in the
manner that you think is most meaningful in reports
to your own legislative body, so that they will
have some basis of evaluating the effectiveness of your
office. Although we have established some priorities,
we have not yet tried to set out in quite specific
and measurable terms the objectives of our office.
You have all heard of PPBS. An application of PPBS may
be helpful for us to determine measurements of internal
effectiveness, at least for my use in finding out how
effective we are.

You have to do some real hard thinking about ways of
measuring your effectiveness. I have no ready answer
for this. I haven't gone through the entire thought
process and found out what my internal measurements
should be yet. It is going to take time to develop.
Most of the measurements to date have been subjective,
I think, just looking over the office and seeing
how well you think it's doing. But there should
be some elements you can measure.

Professor Anderson:

I think that perspectives on your effectiveness would

vary according to their source: the legislator's

perspective, a department head's perspective, and

the perspective of a citizen who had walked in with

a complaint. There might be an overlap in their

perspectives, but they would be different. Are you

taking advantage of the opportunity just to ask every-

body who comes in, either by postcard or some other

means that would preserve their anonymity, to tell

you whether they were satisfied with your services,

and with what the department did in response to your

efforts to help them?

We are doing that in Iowa with a postcard. It's very

simple. It asks, were you satisfied with the effort

the Ombudsman made to assist you? Do you feel the

activities of the Ombudsman helped to solve your

problems? Now, I don't say that that is the ideal

form of a postcard, but it is just handed to

everybody or mailed to them when the transaction is

over. It comes back without any identification

except that the address is varied on the front.

A card given to a person who appears to be from a

lower socio-economic strata has a distinct return

address. In that way, you can sort out poor people

from others, and make a better estimate of how helpful the office is to them.

Ombudsman Walton:

I am interested in your relationship with the University.
Has their Department of Sociology offered any assistance
in terms of evaluating the program, of taking a survey,
a before and after kind of thing?

Ombudsman Doi:

No, we have a sociology student working in our office
as an intern for 9 months. She comes in twice a week.
She is working for her Master's degree.

Ombudsman Walton:

But you are never tempted to have somebody go out and,
say, take a random poll in terms of identifying your
office?

Professor Anderson:

We are trying to get OEO to give us the money. We
would very much like to do precisely that, and hope
that we will be able to do it, but it's not assured
yet.

Complaint-Handling Procedures

Ombudsman Doi:

Your folders contain a flow chart of the procedures
that we follow, the form that we use to take the
initial complaints, and the case status report form,
which enables me to keep up with each case in our
shop. (See Appendix I.)

94

As we have the office organized now, I have one staff person assigned each day to handle complaints for that day. So, he takes all complaints that come in on that one particular day.

Ombudsman Walton:
Is there any prescreening,   such as through the secretary or receptionist?

Ombudsman Doi:
All calls come through the secretary, but she does no screening whatsoever. Whoever the person is in charge of handling complaints that day takes the call. He then decides whether the complaint is within our jurisdiction, whether it is a request for information, or whether it is a complaint in the true sense of the word. The system that we have is relatively simple because the exclusions that we have in our act are rather specific. It is easy to make the determination.

As an additional check, all cases which are handled by that person go across my desk within that week, and I see whether or not it is truly a no-jurisdiction case, or an information case, or a complaint case. So, that's a check to see whether it has been properly classified and properly disposed of.

In the case of a complaint, the person will take the
complaint, he'll reduce it to writing if it's going
to be in letter form, and then the letter comes across
my desk. Each piece of correspondence going out of
our office comes across my desk; each piece of
correspondence coming into the office goes across my
desk. This way, I am able to keep up with whatever
is happening on each case within our shop.

In the no-jurisdiction cases we make a referral to an
appropriate agency or person, but oftentimes we go
beyond that. Especially in the case where you have a
person who really doesn't know what to do. Then we
take the extra time to make the contact for him, and
refer him to a specific person who can handle his
problem.

Informational kinds of inquiries can take a lot of time.
We had a request by a woman about a piece of land above
her house which a developer wanted to develop. She
wanted to know what a citizen could do to prohibit the
development. We spent literally hours researching the
problem--where the development was at that particular
time, what additional permits had to be obtained, what
hearings were going to be held--and then gave her the

entire background of the case, step by step, and
indicated at which point she could make some impact
on stopping the development. Which she did. She
was really happy that she had finally found a governmental agency that responded to her request.

Ombudsman Walton:
Initially, had you referred her to the planning department, would she have been able to get it from them?

Ombudsman Doi:
She really did not know where to go. She knew the
development was going to take place, but she was
not even certain at what stage the development was.
The developer had just announced his plans to develop
the area. We didn't even know where it was. We had
to check ourselves. It can take hours of research
in order to furnish the kind of information that is
meaningful.

We even had a case of Cable TV, which is not within
our jurisdiction, but which was stopped by the
Federal govenment. We had to go to Washington to our
Senators and Representatives to get the information
for the person who had asked for it. So really, the
informational inquiry is not limited to cases within
our jurisdiction, and we try to furnish as much

information as we possibly can get.

Now again, I think this involves a question of priorities.
If you have the time then you can do it. We have found
that the informational requirements are increasing by
leaps and bounds, and this is the reason why we
suggested that they establish an information office
in the Governor's Office.

When the staff member gets a complaint, he fills out
the form that we have for complaint. (See Appendix I.)
He categorizes it, and fills out all of the allegations
that the complainant has told him about. He has to be
a pretty good questioner, to know what information to
obtain in order to get the case resolved.

Ombudsman Walton:
Do you have a syllabus or a format to guide the
questioner?

Ombudsman Doi:
I think he learns by experience.

Every new case that comes in during the week is discussed on the following Monday among all the staff
members, so that we know what cases came in, even if
they were no-jurisdiction or informational cases. It

is discussed among the staff members so that there
will be no repeats. If we had a similar case in the
past, we can go immediately to the files and extract
the information. If it is a case involving a complaint
which someone else has handled he will make reference
to a case file which the staff member may go to for
some leads. If there are questions and facts that have
not been covered in the initial interview, the staff
member is made aware at that time in the discussion
of the case.

Professor Anderson:
That is a compensation for the other decision you made
about not having specialists. You don't want to lose
the expertise; therefore, you have to meet regularly
so that person A can benefit from the previous experience
of person B in a similar case.

Ombudsman Doi:
It all relates back to what you think is the most
efficient way of handling your office, and this
relates back again to the expenditures of my time.
My time is spent basically in reviewing the cases as
they are being handled, and also in reviewing the
recommendations that are being made to me by the staff
members on what I should do. I'm not starting with a
case cold; I have a recommendation from my staff members

in front of me at the time that I am deciding which way we should go on a particular issue.

Professor Anderson:
And this maintains the office as a personal rather than a bureaucratic office.

Professor Moore:
It took about a year for you to develop that system, and to obtain a staff sufficient to enable you to perform a managerial function rather than handling individual cases.

Ombudsman Doi:
During the first year I was handling the managerial function, I was handling individual complaints, I was doing the speeches and all the rest of it, and that is the kind of situation you all are going to face. After the first year, I was about ready to quit.

Mr. Liston:
Apparently most of your complaints come in over the phone, is that correct?

Ombudsman Doi:
Roughly 70% of all complaints.

Mr. Liston:
Do you have an answering service for calls that come in after 5, between 5 in the evening and 8 in the morning?

Ombudsman Doi:

No. We observe regular office hours. Well, usually our staff members are here until six o'clock every evening.

Ombudsman Walton:

When you have an overload, do you ask the receptionist to have them call back, or do you stack them up?

Ombudsman Doi:

We will call back, or if he is busy in a situation where it cannot wait, then he is referred to another staff member.

Ombudsman Walton:

Do you have any evening sessions during the week at all?

Ombudsman Doi:

We have been running on regular governmental schedules simply because there isn't much that you can do when all the governmental offices are shut down, except do the research and the readings that are necessary.

Professor Anderson:

The fact that people can complain by telephone, it seems to me, does make it easier for them even if they are at work--they have a coffee break or a luncheon break when they can call in.

Ombudsman Doi:

Plus, you get calls at home at night. My telephone number is listed in the phone book, so I get calls at night.

BRUCE B. MASON

So, after he gets the initial complaint, then it's the analyst's job to quickly screen whatever rules and regulations are involved, so he can pose the right questions for the agency involved if we correspond with them in writing. And, if we don't, then he still needs this background in order to ask the appropriate questions of the agency to get the response by phone.

Ombudsman Walton:
Do most of those inquiries of the agencies go by phone or by written communication?

Ombudsman Doi:
It depends on the complexity of the complaint. If it is rather complex, or if you figure you are going to have problems later on with proof, you had better put it in writing. If it is a relatively simple complaint, we have been handling it by phone.

The agencies feel we should use the phone more. If we do correspond in writing, then a copy of the correspondence goes to the complainant himself, so that he may review what we have said about what he has told us, to be sure that we have stated the facts correctly. In some instances we have had communication back from the complainant telling us that we did not state the facts exactly as he had related them to us.

In which case we have corrected the letter and sent
it on to the department. So, this provides a check
on our accuracy, and it also serves as a means of notifying the complainant that we are handling his complaint.

Professor Anderson:
Have you got many back marked, "No such person at this
address?"

Ombudsman Doi:
If that happens, we close the case at that point. It
is our policy that we do not handle anonymous complaints, for basically two reasons. One is the danger
of their making all kinds of frivolous allegations.
The second, and more important, is that there is no
way that you can get additional facts from the complainant. What we have been doing is, if the person
does not want to give us his name and address and phone
number, we have taken the complaint and we have
turned it over to the administrator for his information,
with the understanding that we are not investigating
the case, but that he may deal with the complaint as
he wishes. He may want to check up on it himself.
This is a valuable source of information for him.

Then, the agency responds with the facts and documents
that we asked for. In each piece of correspondence we
ask very specific questions about the kind of facts that

we want, and kinds of documents that we want. They
send it back to us, and the time period in between can
stretch out for quite a long time. We have instituted
a reminder system to the agency, where we have sent
them reminders to the effect that we have a complaint
outstanding and we have not received any response.
These reminders are sent about two weeks after the
initial correspondence.

Councilman Tuai:
Are these all addressed to the department head?

Ombudsman Doi:
That's right. Going to the department head is predicated
on several grounds. One, the department head should
know what complaints are being registered against his
department. Secondly, we found that the department
head has a much broader view of what can be done in a
given situation. It is much easier for him to resolve
the problem than if you are dealing with a person way
down the line. The department head has much more
discretion, and he has a broader view of the
community's needs than does the guy who is doing the
actual work down the line.

Ombudsman Walton:
Do you send copies of that letter to anybody else?

Ombudsman Doi:

In all cases on the state government level, a copy of
that letter goes to the Governor's office, at his
request. The statute does not require the office to
do this, but he asked that he be kept informed of
what is happening to the complaints.

Ombudsman Walton:

I assume by the same token that he would get a copy of
the reply from the department.

Ombudsman Doi:

He should.

After the agency responds, the facts and documents are
reviewed by the staff member. Then he begins his
research into the laws, rules, and regulations and
anything else that may be necessary. Let me give you
one example that does not involve law. We had a
complaint about an examination administered by one
of our boards or commissions.   One of my staff members
is presently doing research on what constitutes a good
examination, and one of the things that we have to determine is the fairness of the examination. Since we
do not have that kind of expertise, we are suggesting
that the department and the industry get together to
select a board of review, composed of experts in the
field, to determine whether the examination is fair
or not.

So, after the research is done, the staff members then
make a recommendation to me as to what we should do in
that particular case. At that point, I review the
entire case file along with the recommendation. If
the complaint is deemed justified, then we go through
the appropriate procedure; if not, then the complainant
is notified and the reasons why the complaint is not
justified are given to him. At that point, the case
is closed as far as we are concerned.

Ombudsman Walton:
Do you do this by a form, basically, or through
correspondence?

Ombudsman Doi:
Correspondence. And, the department is notified at
the same time the case is closed. That is to keep
their record-keeping straight.

Ombudsman Walton:
How do you handle complaints by state employees against
their own bureau? Do they remain anonymous?

Ombudsman Doi:
The general policy in our office is that if the name
of the complainant is unimportant to the case, his name
is never released. In the case of a generalized complaint in regard to certain things that the department
is doing, the name of the complainant is not given.

In most cases you will find the name of the complainant
would have to be released, because you are talking
about a specific incident that happened on a specific
date. In order to get the facts and the information that
is necessary, you are going to have to release the
person's name.

Ombudsman Walton:
Do you get many complaints from officials within the
state agencies about their own agencies?

Ombudsman Doi:
We have had a few like that. But I think in most
cases what happens is that if the administrator feels
that he has a type of complaint where he can go no
further in satisfying the complainant, but he feels
that the complainant may have a pretty good case, he
will tell the person to come to us, but not to tell us
that he told him to do so. We have had that happen to
us.

Ombudsman Walton:
Do you have cases from governmental employees dealing
with what they feel would be unfair practices in that
they were not promoted?

Ombudsman Doi:
When it involves hours of work, promotion schedules and
job classification and this kind of thing, we would

classify it as being basically a grievance. We would
advise the complainant to seek the services of his
employee union or organization, or utilize the internal
grievance procedures that are available to him.

Ombudsman Walton:
Would you ever act as an appeals board to the internal
grievance procedure?

Ombudsman Doi:
We are by law told to do so, in that our statute says
that even if the decision is final, we may still review
it. But in that case the test becomes a little different.
If there is reason for the decision that is rendered
by the review board, to my way of thinking that is
sufficient. So the investigation you are conducting
is actually a review of the record before the board
and the reasons stated for the decision.

Mr. Kaye:
Can a complaint be made in other than English?

Ombudsman Doi:
Yes, but we have a hard time in translating what
some complainants are saying. We have had some cases
where all the person could do was speak Japanese.
The problem isn't as critical now. I think most people
are able to converse in English.

Mr. Kaye:
In some other states that wouldn't be the case.

Ombudsman Doi:
In Alberta they have interpreters on the staff.
They have Russians, Poles and all kinds of ethnic
backgrounds.

Professor Anderson:
New Brunswick is bilingual, with French and English.

Mr. Douglas:
In Newark, you would need Spanish-speaking.

Ombudsman Doi:
We have not had the language problem. There has always
been someone who was able to talk to us in English.

Professor Anderson:
Herman, do you get many referrals by attorneys of their
clients to you?

Ombudsman Doi:
Yes.

Ombudsman Walton:
Do you ever have attorneys that come in on behalf of
a client?

Ombudsman Doi:
Yes.

Ombudsman Walton:
Do you insist that the client come in, too?

Ombudsman Doi:
Yes.

Councilman Tuai:

Have you ever reached a situation where an attorney
is involved, and during the course of your investigation he files a law suit?

Ombudsman Doi:

At that point, we would drop it. Once a case is
presented to the court, we no longer have jurisdiction
over that case. We defer to the courts for their
final judgment.

Ombudsman Walton:

Do you ever get second-party complaints, someone complaining on behalf of somebody else?

Ombudsman Doi:

Yes, we have had those and we have told the person,
would you please have the individual who has the
complaint call us, because we know that in getting a
second hand complaint, you are not going to get the
facts. You are going to have permutations of the
facts, but not the exact incident.

What we have done in dealing with a fairly complex
complaint, where there are many legal issues or many
documents involved, is to deliberately ask the person
to come in and visit with us. This has its place, in
the sense that when you are talking to a person
face to face, you tend to know which questions to

ask next, just by his facial response and his uncomfort-
ableness.

Ombudsman Walton:

Don't you find sometimes that their story changes
radically when they are actually face to face with
you and had to tell you the story?

Ombudsman Doi:

That's right.

Resolving Justified Complaints

Ombudsman Doi:

If the complaint is deemed justified, our statute
requires that we informally meet with the agency
involved, or with the person involved in the allegation.

At this stage, I think it is very important that we
have the case so well documented that there is very
little room for doubt as to the outcome of the case.
We have had conferences with numerous administrators.
The thing I like most is when the administrator
throws up his hands and says, "Well, you know more
about our procedures than we do. What do you want
us to do?" At that stage the complaint can be
voluntarily rectified, in most cases. And this is
what has happened in practically all the cases that
we have handled so far. There are very few formal
recommendations that are made by our office. It is
much easier to sit down informally with the department

111

head, so you can observe whether you are making an impact or whether you are not making an impact. One of the systems we have tended to use is to put everything on the blackboard, all of the facts of the case, what procedures have you followed, what is the proposed recommendation, and then go point by point and get agreement. If they say yes, then we get to the recommendations, but by the time you get there you have already sewed up the case.

Professor Anderson:
This is also a tendency in some jurisdictions to submit the recommendation tentatively and preliminarily to the agency with the implied question, "Can you live with this?" Then you get some negotiating. The Ombudsman becomes a broker, you might say, negotiating a settlement between the complainant and the agency. He will himself make decisions as to how much the department can take or cannot take, so you may sometimes sacrifice the complainant's maximum position to some consideration for the efficiency of the agency.

Ombudsman Doi:
The funny thing about this function, you know, is that when you initially get the complaint, you are an objective intermediary, a third party to the complaint. Once you have done the fact-finding and

112

investigation and the research to back up the proposed
recommendations you are going to make and once you decide
on a recommendation, at that point you change into an
advocate. You are now advocating a position. You take
a position.

Ombudsman Walton:
One of the descriptions of an Ombudsman is a citizen's
advocate.

Ombudsman Doi:
You are not an advocate until the time you find the
complaint is justified.

Professor Anderson:
And then you are an advocate for the position, and
not for the person.

Ombudsman Doi:
I cannot underline enough the fact that you have to do
your investigation, you have to do your research before
you are even in a position to think of recommendations.
If it is necessary to make a formal recommendation,
where we cannot agree at the informal conferences as
to what is to be done, then we reduce the recommendation
to writing, and we may or may not stipulate a time
period within which we would like to see the recommendation implemented.

If the agency head has decided that he does not want

to implement our recommendation, he has recourse
by replying to us in writing, giving us the reasons
why he will not implement the decision or the recommendation we have given. If that happens then we will re-
evaluate the case at the time we receive his response,
and if we still feel that we are right we may well go to
publication.

Ombudsman Walton:
At the informal discussion, if the end result is that
you are correct and the department head gives up, then
what notification do you send the complainant?

Ombudsman Doi:
Whatever is decided upon is related to us by the
department in writing. He tells us what he will do to
rectify the complaint. A copy of that letter is
transmitted to the complainant so that he knows
what has happened to his particular complaint.

Ombudsman Walton:
And that closes the file?

Ombudsman Doi:
That may or may not close the file. You want to be
sure that he implements the decision that he has told
us about.

Senator Schmit:
How do you know that?

Ombudsman Doi:
By rechecking.

Senator Schmit:
Do you try to go back and check on every one?

Ombudsman Doi:
Not on every one. In most cases there is no doubt
that it can be implemented right away and there is no
problem about it. In some cases it is necessary to go
back, as where the agency has said, O.K. we'll put out
an informational booklet of some kind in order to
preclude the recurrence of this problem. We go back
and see that it is published.

Ombudsman Walton:
Has the satisfaction requested every been some type of
an apology from an individual?

Ombudsman Doi:
We have had discourtesy complaints on the part of
complainants which we have been able to rectify.

Professor Moore:
Herman, I wonder if you might speculate a little bit
on what you would do if you encountered a really
tough case. I know you have given some thought to
the problem that may arise someday if you can't
get cooperation from a department, how you would go about
dealing with that situation.

Ombudsman Doi:

We have already done our research and have the appropriate forms if we ever have to use a subpoena. Also, we
have whatever forms we have to use in filing our case
in Court to have our subpoena enforced in cases where
it is not adhered to. I think some of the departments
know about it; the Attorney General's Office I am sure
does.

Professor Moore:

That would help you get the information. What about the
use of publicity, which is normally the gun behind the
door? What if you felt the time had come to bring the
gun out?

Ombudsman Doi:

Well, my feeling is that a weapon is good only as
long as it is not used. Once you fire it and it
misfires, it is no longer a weapon. I think I have
to pick and choose the ground on which I am going to
use publicity as an ultimate weapon. And if I use
it, I want to be sure that the person I use it against
will be killed the first time, and not just wounded.
I have to pick and choose the case.

Self-Initiated Investigations
Mr. Douglas:

Do you ever initiate your own investigation, of something you have just generally observed in various complaints that you have received?

As far as an extension of a complaint is concerned,
yes, we have gone beyond the immediate complaint.
In that sense, we have gone on our own motion, trying
to look at the problem much deeper than the original
complaint and just the immediate solution for that
particular individual. We have found in some cases
that the law may have caused inequities, in which
case we have made recommendations to the Legislature
telling exactly why it is inequitable. So we have
recommended legislation.

As far as taking cases purely on our own option, we
have not gotten to that position as yet, for several
reasons. One, we did not find sufficient staff time
to get involved in that area. The other thing I
think that is causing some hesitancy on our part is
that we have enough problems as it is without
getting involved in any new problems that we don't
have to tackle immediately. My concern at the present
time is that I want to establish a solid basis for the
existence of the Ombudsman office in Hawaii. I think
to go out on our own motion is asking for trouble
before the establishment of the institution.

Mr. Douglas:
Would you eventually like to have the staff and the time

to do that kind of thing?

Ombudsman Doi:

Very definitely. In fact, many of my staff members are
getting pretty impatient about not going on our own
motion. I think that is the more interesting kind of
case to investigate.

Relationships With Public Officials
Ombudsman Doi:
Coming now to the other kind of decision that has to
be made--the relationships you're going to have with
administrators, legislators, and all the rest of it--
I think an Ombudsman has to understand legislators,
and legislators have to understand him, in the sense
that you are not going to take your orders from them
in deciding any case. However, I think you have to
understand that they are going to make the appropriations for you. They are going to have to stand back
of you when it gets rough. Your relationship with the
legislators is to a large extent going to determine how
effective you are with administrators, because if
they feel you have the backing of the legislators they
are much more apt to respond, and to voluntarily
rectify.

Professor Anderson:

You are now suggesting that one of the first things an
→Ombudsman has to do is to make contacts with administrators, legislators, unions, and other complaint-handling

mechanisms. How did you go about doing that? Of
course I know Hawaii is a face-to-face community, so
you probably knew a lot of these people.

Ombudsman Doi:
In the case of the unions, we ran across a grievance
which the union had been unsuccessful in resolving,
and we resolved it. The union had called it to my
attention, and suggested that perhaps we had better
get together. So we did. And this led to our
contacts with the other unions, knowing that this
same problem could occur with any employee group.
But it was fortunate that the first case that we
ran across involved a very reasonable union head.

Professor Anderson:
They wanted to have a chance to solve it before you
solved it, is that the idea?

Ombudsman Doi:
No, they were unable to resolve it, so one of their
members came to us as a complainant. We went through
the entire case, and finally found a legal basis.
We told the department that we wanted to have an
official opinion from the Attorney General's office,
knowing what the outcome was going to be, by having
done our legal research. The Attorney General
came out with a ruling substantiating our position, and

payment was made.

After I took office, I asked the Governor for an
opportunity to meet with his cabinet, and he set aside
one day for me to talk to the cabinet, to explain
our role. At that time, all the cabinet members were
there, so we were sure that each department head knew
what we were going to do, and how we were going to do
it.

After that, we did the same thing with the Mayor and
his department heads on the city level. Following
that, we went around to each department, met department heads and their division heads and talked to
them as to what our role was going to be. We did this
for all 18 departments in the state. It was a kind of
joint meeting in which they would tell us what their
problems were, and we would tell them what our problems
were. There was feedback both ways. We were not just
making a speech to them. It was fortunate that I
knew most of the department heads personally, and
I had been in contact with most of the division heads
before becoming Ombudsman, so it really was not a
traumatic experience.

Ombudsman Walton:

Regarding your relationship with the Governor, have
you taken any special steps in dealing with him?

Ombudsman Doi:

After I was appointed he invited me for breakfast.
He invited Senator Kawasaki and myself, and we had a
long informal talk. He expressed his opinion on what
he wanted us to do, and how he wanted us to do it.
He wanted me to hire police investigating officers on
my staff. I told him, "No, I am not going to operate
my office as an investigating unit of that type,
but I am planning to hire pretty high level people so
they can use their judgment and their reasonableness
and their humaneness in handling people." I think the
experiment has worked out pretty well, from the standpoint that he is not bothering us about hiring
investigators. But his own training was in police
work; he is a former policeman.

In fact, after my appointment he assured me that he
would give me his full cooperation and that of his
department heads. I took advantage of that by asking
for a meeting with his cabinet. After the first year,
I again asked him for a chance to talk with his cabinet
to see whether or not there were any ways in which
we could improve our operations, and he allowed us to

do that. We laid it on the line, and told them
"Okay, whatever we have been trying that is wrong,
tell us."

Department heads feel pretty free. When they think we
are overstepping our bounds, they will pick up the
phone and call.

Professor Moore:
In connection with your relationship with the Governor,
it is worth noting that although this is an office
established by the Legislature--with no provision for
any kind of formal clearance or endorsement of either
the office or of the appointment to the office by the
Governor--there was an informal exchange of information
between the Legislature and the Governor before
Herman was appointed. I would not use the word
"clearance," because that would not quite accurately
characterize it. But the Governor was informed of
who the nominee would likely be, and had an opportunity
at that point to say that he didn't think very much
of that idea, or to say it was all right.

Ombudsman Doi:
As any Governor, he has votes in the Legislature.

Ombudsman Walton:
Have you had any complaints concerning the Attorney
General's office?

Ombudsman Doi:

Not about the Attorney General himself, but about
some of his staff, like the Sheriff's office, for
example, in connection with Sheriff's processes.

The Attorney General has been very cooperative. In
fact, in some of our recommendations, in some of our
advice to the departments, we deliberately tell them
"If I were in your position I would seek an Attorney
General's opinion." In which case, the department
head then directs an inquiry to the Attorney General's
office and gets back an opinion. In some cases, we
have gone directly to the Attorney General and asked
him for an opinion on interpreting certain laws for
the direction of the department. This was the case
with the Public Utilities Commission, as to whether
they should pay interest on deposits or not. They
came out with an opinion substantiating ours.

Councilman Tuai:

Is the Attorney General elected?

Ombudsman Doi:

He is appointed.

Mr. Kaye:

Herman, have you ever had a complaint to investigate
a Community Action Agency?

Ombudsman Doi:

No, we have not. We have had a complaint against
the OEO office about the Kona project, on the island
of Hawaii, but after an investigation we found he did
not have much of a complaint. The then director coopera-
ted fully with us.

The theory here has been that we extend our jurisdiction
as far as possible. I feel that we can always go
back. If you limit yourself initially, you are going
to be less effective.

Professor Moore:

Were your relationships with the administration complicated by the rivalry between the Lt. Governor
and the Governor?

Ombudsman Doi:

Sure. But we managed to weather that storm. One of
the prime rules I had during the last election, when
my former law partner--who was then Lt. Governor of
the State--ran against an incumbent Governor, was
that I had to decide whether I was going to be an
Ombudsman or whether I was going to be a political
animal. If I had decided to be a political animal,
I would have quit my job. I would have resigned,
and taken up the campaign. But, as it was, I remained
in the job and tried to see the job through. There
was no campaigning on my part. I stayed completely

away from the campaign.

Controlling Growth and Work-Load

Senator Schmit:

One of the charges made against the establishment of
the office in Nebraska was that the office itself
would become just one more stage of bureaucracy. Do
you anticipate the expansion of your office, and to
what extent, and how far removed will you yourself be
from the complaints?

Ombudsman Doi:

I don't expect our office will exceed more than six
professional people. I'm not sure right now. We have
only a year-and-nine-months' experience, but it seems
that the number of complaints is levelling off. Now
whether or not this is a true picture, or whether it's
going to pick up in the next year or not, I'm not
sure. But in any case, once we get to six, we are
going to be limited by our physical facilities.
I can't see building another bureaucracy, personally.
I think the office has to remain personal in the sense
that every decision that is made is a decision that
I can agree with.

Senator Schmit:

This is my concept. I felt one of the reasons why it
works in a state the size of Hawaii or Nebraska is
because it does not need to be a staff of 40 people.

125

Ombudsman Walton:

Denmark still has seven professionals, in addition to the Ombudsman and they cover the whole nation. It hasn't really grown by more than a couple since its origin. Something that is quite interesting is that the Ombudsman still reviews every single case. He makes **every** decision.

Ombudsman Doi:

Putting a complaint in writing is a means of reducing the number of complaints.

Ombudsman Walton:

Well, that's true, they do have the requirement of submitting complaints in writing.

Professor Moore:

Herman, if you found that your department was over-taxed, that you were getting more complaints than you felt you could handle, how would you go about adjusting the volume of complaints to the capacity of your staff?

Ombudsman Doi:

Initially, we were really being overtaxed and seriously considered the possibility that I might have to weed out complaints--just send letters to the people saying "We got your complaint, but we are sorry we cannot pursue it any further simply because time is not available," and screen them on the basis of a very perfunctory look at the complaint itself--scale of importance, etc. But, fortunately, as the complaints grew in number, I was able to add additional staff members. Last session, we had the position ceiling removed. If that had not been done, I was seriously thinking of limiting complaints to the more important ones.

Professor Moore:
And, of course, you have already referred many complaints to the Office of Information and Complaint.

Ombudsman Walton:
Could you have simply referred more of those near the gray area to the other agencies?

Ombudsman Doi:
That is another possibility, sure. You can fall back on jurisdiction at the same time.

Professor Wyner:
What if you had stopped speaking at all the Kiwanis clubs, high schools, police recruits, etc.?

Ombudsman Doi:
I would not have sacrificed that portion, really. The information dissemination is really an important function of the Ombudsman. The funny thing about people is that they don't want me to send my deputy out, they want me to come, and this places a real

burden on the person having to personally appear all
the time. Listening to yourself often enough gets very
boring.

Professor Moore:
You wouldn't be inclined to require that complaints be
submitted in writing?

Ombudsman Doi:
That is a possibility, but I would take that as a
really last resort. That would be a real deprivation
to certain elements of our community.

Ombudsman Walton:
As opposed to that, you could invite them in and have
a secretary to whom they could dictate their complaint.

Comparisons With Other Jurisdictions

Professor Anderson:
What was the timing of your trip to Scandinavia?

Ombudsman Doi:
Let's see, I went in the latter part of September,
1969, so I'd been in office about three months. I
went to Canada last year, 1970. I wanted to go
initially to Scandinavia because that is where it
all started--to look at the system in terms of
its history and what they had done. They had the
longest experience. Then, you could play around
with permutations of that system, to fit into your
own situation.

Professor Anderson:

If you were to go back now, do you think you might
have a different perspective and different kinds of
questions to ask?

Ombudsman Doi:

Very definitely so. I'd be less concerned about
processing, the procedures to be followed, or staffing
problems, or with the organization of the office.
Now I'd be more concerned with relationships, the
kinds of problems that are encountered and how they
are solved, with inspection trips and how they are
conducted. I was interested in those problems when
I went there, but I have many more questions than I
had when I originally went. Also, in making a decision
to proceed on your own motion, how you make this
kind of decision? Those would be the fundamental
kinds of questions that I would ask.

I found something very interesting when I went to
Canada. In talking with the Ombudsman there, we
found that the complaints we were handling and the
problems that we were encountering were very similar.
Although the cases themselves may be different, the
basic problems and the basic kinds of resistance you
get on the part of the administrators and on the
part of the legislators are exactly the same. I

129

guess we are all dealing with human beings, so the
problems are basically the same.

Speaker Beppu:
John, I have a question. If you use Herman's office
as an example of efficiency, productivity, can you apply
this standard in other states or jurisdictions? I'd
like to see the reaction from different people, whether
Herman's experience is transferable.

Professor Wyner:
I can give you one reaction to that. I've just asked
Lt. Governor Paul Simon of Illinois that exact question.
He looked me straight in the eye and said it simply
would not work. The reason for it, he suggested, is
simply the nature of party politics in Illinois.
First thing, he said, we would never get the bill
passed, and if it did get passed, the Ombudsman,
despite what the law says, would continue to depend
upon the political party or faction. If the Governor
or the Mayor of Chicago was down on the Ombudsman
and let it be known that their agency people simply
should not cooperate with him, he's dead.

Professor Moore:
In contrast to this example, Senator Schmit
pointed out that in Nebraska, although they enacted
legislation at almost exactly the same time as you

did in Hawaii, they had greater difficulty in getting
the consensus needed to appoint a man to make it a
functioning office. The experience in Hawaii was very
helpful in reassuring members of the Legislature
that it could perform in a way that would not be
competitive, but would be rather helpful. So there
you have two polar extremes.

Speaker Beppu:
How about the State of California?

Professor Anderson:
The population of 20 million does distinguish
California and a couple of the larger states. How much
workload can the office handle without losing that
personal touch? How much work can that one man keep
track of? You wonder if in California you might not
have to chop it up somehow by regions or by subjects.

One of the things that we want, and that Herman Doi
wants, is to develop uniform categories of case
recording, so that the comparison will be appropriate,
and we won't be talking about apples and pears.
I definitely think that the case recording here will
provide a standard for measurement, and one which
other areas will aspire to attain. I think we are
extremely fortunate, as Herman has heard here before,

that this first office has been so outstanding in its
quality, growing out of the support from the Legislature--
because it was a unanimous appointment. So we have
set a high mark for these other jurisdictions. They
do not necessarily have to attain it completely to be
a good Ombudsman office, but at least they have something to work toward.

COMPLEMENTARY COMPLAINT-HANDLING AGENCIES
Professor Moore:
It is our good fortune this morning to have several
additional guests, including our host in the State
Capitol, the Speaker of the House Tadao Beppu; the
Ombudsman for the University of Hawaii, Charles James;
the Director of the Office of Information and
Complaint for the City and County of Honolulu James
Loomis, and his Assistant Director for Complaints,
Patrick De Costa.

We would like to ask each of the guests for a brief
characterization of his own complaint-handling work,
and of the relationship of that work to the Ombudsman
office. Beginning with you, Speaker Beppu, I think
we would all be interested in your perspective on the
apprehension of some legislators that the Ombudsman
office might compete with their case work and their

132

constituent-relations. Has that apprehension been
reduced? Is the Legislature living comfortably with
the Ombudsman?

The Hawaii State Legislature

Speaker Beppu:

I would say we are comfortable with the Ombudsman's
office. One of the things I have found, and most of
our legislators here have found, is that it takes
away a lot of the workload, because we have experts
in Herman's office that can help us, especially in the
area of legal technicalities. We are very fortunate
in having someone with Herman's background--as former
Chief Clerk of the Committee of Judiciary in the days
of the Territory, as Chief Clerk of the Finance Committee
in the House, and as Director of the Legislative
Reference Bureau. Knowing the State government
inside out, and the county government inside out, he
is able to cope with many of the questions and complaints that come in. Herman's office can explain
the duties of the state legislators and the powers
of the councilmen in the respective counties. I think
he has been very helpful.

Professor Moore:

Do you find that his office provides you--as a
legislator--with the option of pursuing a constituent
complaint within your own office, or of referring it

to Herman's office, depending on its complexity and
whether or not you feel a special obligation to the
constituent?

Speaker Beppu:

We have many referrals to our office, and I can't
tell you how many of them are referred to Herman.
In my case, if I have a hundred calls, I might
refer 10 calls to Herman. Herman doesn't know this,
but I refer all the tough ones to him.

Mr. Kaye:

Mr. Beppu, do you have any idea yet about how fast
your own staff can come up with responses, compared to
how fast Herman's staff can do it?

Speaker Beppu:

I think we are just as fast, or maybe faster. It
depends on the kind of staff you have. We have staff
people who know government, and they can just give
an answer right away over the telephone. We don't
expect people to write letters to us all the time,
or to Herman's office. I think the public appreciates
this.

Professor Moore:

Mr. Speaker, I know you can't speak for all the members
of the Legislature, but perhaps you could characterize
their feeling about the cost of the office. Are they

getting at all concerned about the expense entailed
in supporting an Ombudsman office?

Speaker Beppu:
No, from our end we don't see too much objection to
Herman's budget. We started off with $103,000, which
was the bare minimum. The only time that any questions
about his budget came up was when we raised the pay of
the Ombudsman and the Legislative Auditor to make
them comparable to our Circuit Court Judge's pay.
Because Herman's office was new, he had a small staff
compared to the Legislative Auditor, who had been in
business about five years already and had a big staff.

The question came up from among some of the House
members, why should the office of the Ombudsman have
the same pay as the Auditor? We nullified that
argument by saying that Herman's office had just
started, and the fact that he has five people or
fifty people should not deter them from paying the
kind of salary that the office deserves. But if you
do make a comparison, then the Attorney General should
have the lowest pay in the State, because he has the
least number of people working for him. The Health
Director and the Director of Transportation should have
the highest pay, because they are the biggest departments.

And that's the only time the question of money came in.

Professor Moore:
Do you contemplate continuing its location in the Legislature's budget?

Speaker Beppu:
We have two agencies under our legislative appropriations--the Office of Ombudsman and the Legislative Auditor. We have another agency, the Legislative Reference Bureau, which is also an arm of the Legislature. We put it under the University of Hawaii for administrative purposes, and to give it the kind of independence that that office should have. As long as these offices are part of Legislative Services, we will keep them under our appropriation.

Professor Moore:
When I was here about a year ago, I spoke to some members of the House who indicated they would like to be informed from time to time during the year if there were patterns of complaints evolving within their districts, rather than waiting for an annual report to find out. What do you feel about that? Do you think that that would be proper or desirable?

Speaker Beppu:
I think it would be nice public relations for the

office of Ombudsman, but perhaps if they don't know
about it, they'd be better off as far as their role
as a legislator is concerned. They can't be involved
in every minute complaint that Herman is handling.

Professor Moore:
So it might reduce the value of the office in one way,
if they were continually informed of what was happening?

Speaker Beppu:
Yes. I think the reason we created the office of
Ombudsman is to keep some of the complaints away from
us.

Professor Anderson:
Along that same line, I notice here in the Ombudsman's
First Annual Report, on page 24, there have been
several suggestions to review legislation and several
proposals for revision of legislation. Did the
Legislature find this useful?

Speaker Beppu:
Yes. We appreciate his recommendations. I think one
of the reasons that Herman does this is because of
his background. If he had just been a man off the
streets, I don't think he would go to the extent of
trying to recommend legislation.

Professor Anderson:
So these are suggestions that he's made, in areas like

amending his own statute, registration of vehicles
located outside the state, designation of traffic
control devices, stay of judgment in Workman's
Compensation, and the State Information Office. Was
action ever taken on any of these during the recent
session of the Legislature?

Ombudsman Doi:
Some bills have advanced. Those not completed during
this session will be carried over.

Professor Moore:
The Ombudsman office has been going for nearly two
years now. When the Legislature looks at an
appropriations request from the office, what kinds of
things would it look for in determining whether its
initial confidence has been justified?

Speaker Beppu:
I think the report that comes out, the yearly report,
is self-evident of the kind of work they are doing.
I've never had any complaints about the office of
Ombudsman, and I don't think any legislators have,
and I think this is indicative of the kind of work
the office is doing.

Ombudsman Doi:
Maybe I can help in that respect. Every session we
have to go before the House Finance Committee and the

Senate Ways and Means Committee to substantiate the
request for our appropriations, at which time numerous
questions are asked about case loads and with regard
to specific cases legislators know about, to find
out what the outcomes were. In that sense, they
have a specific feel for what the office is doing.
It's a pretty good hearing in the sense that they take
us through the mill, to be sure that we are not
getting more money than we deserve, that we are
not playing around with cases.

Speaker Beppu:
We have an understanding between the three of us--
the two presiding officers of the House and the
Senate and Herman--that when he wants to pick up a
new staff member, he'll come up and say, look, I
want this man, do you have any objection? And I think
this is important, that we can verify the
kind of staff that he picks up.

Professor Moore:
Now I'd like to ask Jim Loomis and Pat De Costa to
briefly describe the nature of their operation, and
perhaps in the course of that description, to touch
upon the significance you attach to your relationship
with the Mayor, since one of the characteristics of
the Ombudsman office is its independence. Then, you

139

might also respond to the suggestion that your volume
of work has been reduced by the presence of the Ombudsman office, and say something about the working
relationships between the two offices.

The Honolulu Office of Information and Complaint

Director Loomis:

The Office of Information and Complaint for the City
and County of Honolulu is created and dismissed in
the City Charter in one sentence. I'll paraphrase it:
"There shall be attached to the office of the Mayor
the Office of Information and Complaint whose function
shall be to answer inquiries and complaints about
city policies, procedures and so on." This is the
substance of it and that's it, the whole thing.

I think those who drafted the City Charter very
specifically made the point of including my office
within the Mayor's office. The net result is that
our office is only as strong and as effective as
the Mayor wishes it to be. We have two divisions,
as you can tell from the title. We have the
information side of the office and we have the
complaint side of the office. There is a great deal
of overlap.

Theoretically, we have people in our office that are
complaint specialists or investigators. We have other

people who are information specialists, which is
a euphemism for PR men, I guess. But, we find
that everyone, regardless of their title, does
double duty, working in both areas, because the two
areas very often are interwoven. In response to a
complaint, the city will take a particular form of
action and the result is the necessity to dispense
information about that action.

Complaint-Handling and Public Relations
Director Loomis:
We have a terrific volume of work. We categorize the
calls that we respond to as "inquiries and/or complaints,"
and we further distinguish complaints <u>requesting</u>
service from complaints <u>about</u> service. According to
our last quarterly report, it looks as if our volume
for this fiscal year will be about 11,000. We get a
pretty high volume of inquiries--for example, people
wanting to know which city agency they should go to
to get a marriage license. We had a woman call wanting
us to get the fire department to get a stray cat down
from a tree. These are the very simple routine
inquiries and complaints that we can and do handle
with a phone call.

Then, a little further down the scale, we get people
calling because there is water flowing out of a man-hole

in front of their house, or there is a dead cat on the highway, and the city provides a dead animal removal service. This, incidentally leads our list of complaints, the dead animals. And we go all the way down the line, through the people who are having difficulty with city agencies, people who get bogged down with some of the minor bureaucrats in the City and County government, people who through a technicality have been refused a building permit.

We had a man come in a few weeks ago whose business is the installation of mail boxes in front of private homes. He ran into someone in our planning department who uncovered a technicality in our zoning ordinance that if you have a mail box in front of your house with your name on it, it violates the zoning ordinance: It is a sign and it can't be more than a foot square. Well, obviously, this is a technicality in the law that was never intended to apply to a mail box. Pending a revision of the zoning ordinance, we used our office to get to the Building Department, which is charged with enforcement of this zoning ordinance, and we have reached sort of an understanding with the Building Department that in this case they just won't enforce the law until we make the necessary adjustments.

Then, we go all the way down the line to someone who calls in and says he was assaulted by a police officer and is afraid to go to the police department with his complaint for fear that they'll ignore it, whitewash it, or whatever. So that pretty much covers the gamut on the complaint side.

On the information side, we perform the function of a public relations, press relations outlet for the City and County. We write speeches for the Mayor, we answer mail, we take care of the drafting of proclamations, we answer questions from the press, we put the press in touch with city departments, and so on.

We have an extremely busy office, We have nine people on our staff, and thank goodness I'm blessed with a marvellous staff. These people voluntarily come in early and stay late. One of them comes in at 7:00 o'clock in the morning. Frequently, I'm there until 6:30 or 7 o'clock at night. Pat is often there that late, and we frequently work on weekends. So, in effect, we have a live, warm body there almost 12 hours a day.

The balance of the time we have an answering service. The service has a sort of poop sheet that we provided them with, and from that they can handle the routine inquiries and complaints. But Pat or I, or someone on our staff is on call 24 hours a day, so that we really do provide 24-hour, 7 days-a-week service to people who call up.

Professor Anderson:
Would you say that the first time someone calls in to say there is a dead cat in the alley that that's an inquiry or request for service, but that the second time it's a complaint?

Director Loomis:
I would think so. Pat, would you agree with that?

Assistant Director De Costa:
Yes.

Director Loomis:
Hopefully, there won't be a second time, at least for the same cat!

Professor Anderson:
The complaint category in your quarterly report, then, would be people who are literally complaining about some maladministration or failure to do something.

Director Loomis:

This is true, but I sort of rebel against the way this word complaint is tossed around. I suppose a great many of the calls we get that we must arbitrarily classify as a complaint are not what I would call a complaint. They are requests from people who have an immediate problem and they want to expedite that problem. If there is a watchword in our office it is expedite.

Assistant Director De Costa:

We use the word complaint because it attaches some urgency. If you read further on, we break down our complaints into complaints requesting service, and complaints about service and/or policy. (See Appendix III.) Local people have only recently begun to learn how to complain. They always say, I don't like to complain, this isn't a complaint,... Then they give you a complaint!

Director Loomis:

Just to illustrate our dilemma in this area, let me give you an example. About six-thirty, I got a call from a man who said "Somebody's got to help me, there's a cop in my living room and he's about to take me to jail." The problem was that he had to go to Court on a traffic citation, and the day he was supposed to appear in court there was a death in the family, so he called the City Prosecutor and he explained the situation, and the fellow he talked to said "Don't worry about it, we'll take care of it, we'll just give you another court date and we'll notify you by mail." So the man forgot about it and he kept waiting for the letter, but the Prosecutor forgot about it too.

All of a sudden, late one afternoon, a bluecoat showed up at the guy's front door and said "Come on, you're coming with me." Because people are beginning to become aware of what we do, and how we do it, he said, "Just a minute, let me make my one phone call now, rather than when you get me downtown." He called our office and said, "Help me." I told the policeman to stay right there until I got back to him; I got hold of the Prosecutor, he called the officer, and we fixed it up right on the spot. I don't know if you'd call this a complaint, an inquiry, or what.

Ombudsman Tuai:
When you expedite a matter, how long does it generally take?

Assistant Director De Costa:
We try to do as much business as we can on the phone. Accessibility is the main thing. Government is inaccessible to the people. Here in Hawaii, the

Ombudsman function and our Ombudsmanlike function
helps to increase this accessibility. So, we try to
encourage complaints on the phone. Then we encourage
our staff and ourselves to handle them on the phone right
away. If we can do it on the phone, with an appropriate
file kept, the action can be expedited that day or the
next day. If the person didn't have his garbage picked
up this morning, we are not going to send a service
request down to the records division, because they won't
get it until tomorrow. So, we call them.

The Number and Nature of Complaints
Professor Moore:
Just a moment ago, you suggested that as your office
becomes more visible, and as the Mayor's support of the
office becomes more widely known, you are getting more
complaints, which suggests the possibility that these
kinds of services have a built-in tendency to expand.

Director Loomis:
No question about it. We have people who stumble
around and do not know where to call. Finally, they
get to our office and they get immediate action, and
from then on they are steady customers. I think
probably one of the major factors in the way our
office is moving is the personality of the Mayor, who
has established a reputation as a guy who gets things

done, a man of action. People now say, well, I'm having trouble with the Building Department, I'm going to call the Mayor's office, because he'll get it done. Of course, it never gets to the Mayor. It comes right straight to us.

Professor Moore:
Do you think people will get so accustomed to complaining that things may get out of hand?

Director Loomis:
I don't think it will get out of hand. I think there are a very, very small group of chronic complainers. I got my first complaint call at home, one-hour-and-forty-five minutes after my telephone was installed, which will give you an idea of how they get to you. With the exception of this very small group of people, I don't think so. We do get some people who keep coming back, people who regard themselves as sort of private watchdogs. Every time they see a bus driver who is discourteous, every time they see litter on the streets they call us.

Ombudsman Walton:
How do you handle those people?

Director Loomis:
As patiently as possible.

Ombudsman Walton:
You get to know them and identify them.

Director Loomis:
Oh, yes, because this woman who called me at home
the first time, she screamed and yelled. She wanted a
dead dog removed right then, right now. This was
10 o'clock at night. It shook me a little bit. She
hung up on me, after calling me a blood-sucker and a
criminal. It just went on. She was insane, really.
I was still shaken the next morning when I went
into the office and mentioned her name to Pat. He
said, "oh, forget it. We know her. She's one of
our best customers." In her particular case it looks
as if it's working out, because she's had so many
experiences with our people. She won't talk to me,
she won't talk to Clarence Maki, she won't talk to
Bob Lifken. She'll talk to Pat now, but we are
gradually working to the point where she won't talk
to anybody in our office.

Professor Anderson:
Some of these consistent complainers, do they serve a
useful purpose for you?

Director Loomis:
Absolutely. Because in many cases their complaint is
valid. It's their manner that's offensive; their
complaint is not.

Assistant Director De Costa:
We have a guy you probably know, Herman--he's always
parking cars at Charlie's Tavern--and every time we
hear from him there's about a dozen complaints and
inquiries and suggestions we have to reply to,
and a lot of these things are excellent suggestions
that other people have made or maybe other people
have thought about and have not made. On the other
hand, some are just silly. We have gotten to the
point where we can handle him.

Ombudsman Doi:
He came back to our office the other day with a whole
new list of suggestions.

Director Loomis:
Yes, we finally insisted that he write them down, which
is an exception, because in most cases we don't do
this. As I said a minute ago, the watchword in our
office is expedite and the reason for it, frankly,
is because we just have such a terrific volume of work.
We simply don't have time for memos in triplicate.
We just can't.

Councilman Tuai:
Do you have any allegations against police? You don't
have the black problem where you hear the cry that the
police are guilty of brutality?

Ombudsman Doi:
Here we have the white problem. The younger white
segment, the longhaired segment, allege police brutality
much more often than anybody else.

Director Loomis:
If I can judge from this distance what's going on in
mainland cities, it's beautiful here. I think in the
last four months there may have been two or three
complaints of alleged police brutality.

If there appears to be grounds for the complaint after
some superficial checking on my part, then we will
proceed through normal police channels, and the
Police Department has a special Inspection Section
for the investigation of this sort of thing. Then,
depending on a value judgment, myself, Pat, or someone
from our office may participate to an extent in the
investigation, to provide sort of an outside observer
to try to ensure a fair investigation. We have never
had any question about the fairness of an investigation
of this type.

Many of them we can head off ahead of time, if the
complaint obviously has no grounds. I had one a couple
of weeks ago from a man who said he was beat up at 4:30
in the morning. He said "I have a witness," and he gave

me the man's name. I went through the routine business
of calling this witness, and he said, "No, the cop
didn't beat him up, the guy was falling down drunk, he
was hanging around with a couple of prostitutes and
all the policeman did was keep him from falling
down in the gutter and hurting himself. He put him in
a cab and sent him home."

So, obviously, that terminated it. I wrote the complainant a letter and said "I called the witness and
your story was not corroborated, and it does not
appear to me that any further action is necessary."
If he wanted to discuss it further with me, he
could, but that was the end of it. Obviously, there
is no point in sending that on to the Police Department,
because when they investigate, it comes back that thick.

Mr. Douglas:
Is there any way that you or anyone can tell what
percentage of your clients are low-income people?

Director Loomis:
I don't think it would be possible to make any sort
of survey. Furthermore, I don't think the vast
majority of complaints we get have any bearing on that.
A cat can be hit in front of anybody's house. I'm
not sure there would be any way of pinning it down.

Assistant Director De Costa:

It might be interesting from a sociological standpoint. We could do it by area, if we had a research
person in our office. Off hand, I think it just
runs the gamut of people.

Mr. Douglas:

Isn't there a tendency of lower income people not to
be informed, or just so apathetic that they don't
think it's worthwhile trying to complain?

Ombudsman Doi:

That is changing in Hawaii, insofar as the poor are
getting organized.

Director Loomis:

I think you'll find, generally, that the people here
are much more involved. In a nonpresidential year,
we'll get an 89% to 90% election turnout.

Mr. Douglas:

Do you have any special type of information system to
reach out to the poor?

Assistant Director De Costa:

Yes, through the Federal Model Cities program,
housing information and other information centers
have been set up in the poverty pockets, and have proved
successful. It seems to me something like that could
be funded at the State and city level and expanded
beyond the Model Cities target areas.

Ombudsman Doi:

I think the workers in the area are aware of the
existence of both of our programs, and I am sure
they are making referrals. When they run across
problems, they are sending people to us.

Director Loomis:

I think the work of our office is pretty well publicized.
People know where we are and what we do. For those
of you who are not from Honolulu or from Hawaii, we
have a disc jockey in the morning here who has most
of the audience, and frequently somebody will call
and say, "Hey, something has happened, my trash wasn't
picked up," or whatever. He tells them, "Well, call
Jim Loomis down at City Hall," which makes me cringe
a little with a quarter-of-a-million people listening.
But, we get plenty of publicity.

Professor Anderson:

Does HOIC ever get complaints from city employees
about their employment conditions or promotions?

Director Loomis:

We get complaints from city employees calling as
private citizens.

Professor Anderson:

I wasn't thinking so much of that as their working
conditions, whether they get promoted or passed
over, their hours, how their supervisor treats them.

Not too often. We had one recently where a building
inspector said he was intimidated by an applicant.
The guy came in for a building permit, and because
he couldn't get this processor to act the way he wanted,
the guy intimidated him. So the building inspector
got all shook up and he came up to our office to
complain about this member of the general public.
We didn't do anything about it, because the employee
did not want to file a formal complaint. He just
wanted to know what he could do, what were his rights.
We explained them to him. He chose not to do
anything about it, with the understanding that if it
happened again that he would know what to say, how
to conduct himself, what his rights were. Then, should
the applicant persist, we could become involved if
the complainant wanted to actually become a witness
and file a charge.

Another area is promotions. Very often people in the
department hear scuttlebutt about promotions. After
we have made an investigation, we find out the facts
and we can report to the complainant. If he wants to
be anonymous, we have this ruling in our office that
we will hold his name in confidence so the department
shall not know. The person is a member of the depart-

ment, but the department head does not know who is complaining. That way you reduce the possibility of reprisal.

Director Loomis:

A fireman was active in his campaigning against our Mayor, and as a result one of the officials above him-- sort of in retaliation--transferred this guy. He lived at Hawaii Kai, and worked at the fire station there, and they transferred him. So he complained to us, and we went to the Mayor, and the Mayor had him moved right back again.

Forestalling Recurrent Complaints

Professor Anderson:

We are very interested in a special segment of your work, although we realize that you do a lot of other things. Take for example, this gentleman with the policeman in his living room. Well, it was an oversight; this could happen to anyone. In other words, there was nothing you could do to remedy a recurring situation. If you had had a dozen of these, you'd figure they'd better set up some procedure. What I want to ask is, most of your cases you can solve by getting the animal removed or what have you, but how many of them give you an opportunity to go in and correct the situation that leads to complaints?

153

Director Loomis:
Quite a few. Of course, every time we handle a complaint, in the back of our minds is the idea, is
there anything to this one incident that may indicate
a basic problem there?

Professor Anderson:
What channels of communication do you use when you
identify a case of that kind?

Director Loomis:
The appropriate department. If it's public works, we
go to the Public Works Department.

Professor Anderson:
You go to the top instead of the bottom?

Director Loomis:
Oh yes.

Assistant Director De Costa:
Let me give you a simple example. Two years ago,
cesspool complaints were number one. People would
call in and say, I asked for my cesspool to be pumped
and it wasn't pumped. We get to the yard and the
yard says we pumped that cesspool. There is no way
to prove it, because the guy wasn't home, the neighbours
were not around. So, we devised a little doorhanger.
When the cesspool is pumped, the guy who pumped it signs
his name, the date and the time and the level of the
cesspool, so when the resident gets home he knows that

the cesspool was done. Because if it rains, if
there is a bad soil condition, the cesspool may over-
flow again a few hours later, and he may feel he never
got serviced.

Professor Anderson:
So cesspool complaints are now down to number two
on your list of 10?

Assistant Director De Costa:
Yes. In the winter time, you know, with the soil
conditions we have here water comes in to the cesspools
as fast as you pump them out.

Ombudsman Doi:
Perhaps a better example is the system you set up for
bulk trash collection. Now they have systematic
pickups in different areas, where before they used
to respond to special calls and you just couldn't
keep up with the number of calls that were coming in.
A system was devised after numerous complaints were
received.

Assistant Director De Costa:
We make a conscious effort to eliminate complaints
before they happen. We had a hand in trying to set
up some of these procedures in advance. For the first
time, the Planning Department put out part of their
budget in advance to community associations around the

island where there was a project affecting that area.
We have assisted in setting up and running public
hearings where the issue involved was fairly controversial, or could have been fairly controversial.
And this is where you start to get a sort of melding
of our complaint and information functions. On the
surface you could make a case for two separate offices,
an information office and a complaint office. But
I don't feel that way. At least in our case, I think
it has worked better because so many times, in a
public relations sense, if you take action in that
capacity you're going to forestall complaints
that might be coming in if we didn't.

I take the complaint side as being customer relations.
I have an example on changing procedures. We had
a major policy change which was recommended by our
office last year and this had to do with zoning
violations. The Planning Department has always
enforced its own code, and they were backlogged with
people who had made complaints a year ago because they
had only two inspectors and because they had to handle
"more important things" than zoning violations such
as two families in a single-family residence, or
raising chickens in a residential area. So, what

happened was that we made a recommendation to the
Mayor, and the Mayor made the necessary administrative
change; this is an advantage of having the strong
mayor type of government that we have. Following
our recommendation, the Mayor took the enforcement of
zoning violations out of the Planning Department, and
put it in with the Building Department, which had
an increase in staff last year and which can more
properly handle the situation. Now these zoning
violations are moving faster. The backlog has been
cut down considerably, and the building inspectors
actually do a better job because they are very
professional people who are top-notch inspectors. The
zoning code is related to the plumbing, electrical,
building and housing code work that they do anyway.

*Relationships With the Ombudsman and
Other State Agencies*

Ombudsman Doi:
Are there certain kinds of complaints that you refer to
Herman's office?

Director Loomis:
If it involves a state agency. I would say we refer
very few complaints to you, Herman. In most cases we
try to help. That is paramount. So, if someone is
calling with a problem that involves a state agency,

rather than just say, "We are not involved, call
this department instead," many times, most times,
we will make the call for them and put the two parties
in touch. It is entirely possible that Herman
might have got some feedback after that; the guy
still didn't get satisfaction, so then he goes to
Herman.

Ombudsman Doi:
The working relationship that we have with Jim's office
is excellent, because on every city complaint, their
office is kept informed. Either we go through their
office, or we go directly to the department head, but
a copy of the letter to be sent to the department head
goes to Jim's office.

Ombudsman Walton:
Do you attempt to divide complaints between those that
you feel you should handle and those which his department would handle?

Ombudsman Doi:
No, in every case where there is a complaint against
a City and County official, or a city department,
we either work through Jim or we work with the director
of the department with Jim's knowledge.

Assistant Director De Costa:
About one-fourth of the complaints that you handle,
Herman, are city and county related. A lot of the time

the person, just to cover all bases, complains to
our office and then to your office. There is a
duplication of effort. When there is an active complaint that has not yet been finalized at the city
level, perhaps the Ombudsman can wait.

Ombudsman Doi:
We have been doing that. We lay off and find out
what the final result is. There is no sense in our
calling the department head at the same time.

Assistant Director De Costa:
Yes, our relationship with Herman's office is excellent,
and a lot of times we go in on complaints together.

Professor Moore:
What kinds of complaints?

Assistant Director De Costa:
Police brutality, for example.

Ombudsman Walton:
On the cases where you have a complaint that a person
might think is unsatisfactorily resolved, what does
he do then? Does he go to his councilman, or does
he come to Herman's office?

Director Loomis:
To Herman's office.

*Relationships With Councilmen, the Mayor, and
Administrative Personnel*
Ombudsman Walton:
Do very many of them go to their councilmen?

Director Loomis:

They do. In many cases, the councilman merely refers them to us. Or, the councilman apprises us of the complaint, we arrive at a decision, a solution, an answer, or whatever, and we go back to the councilman, who in turn responds to the complainant.

Ombudsman Walton:

Where they don't think they are being satisfied, do they then go on to the Mayor's office?

Assistant Director De Costa:

We are the Mayor's office. Sometimes when it's a matter of policy change that is beyond us, we have to take it to the Mayor, but very rarely. That's the whole reason for the office. It's like the Speaker said, the service that the Ombudsman provides to the legislators is the same that we provide for all the elected officials, primarily the Mayor. It is a cliché in American government, "Call the Mayor's office, call City Hall." A lot of the City councilmen get complaints, and they give them to us either verbally or in written form. Rather than going directly to the complainant with the final answer, we go back to the councilmen, so the work that we do makes all the elected officials look better in the view of the public.

Ombudsman Walton:

Is there any attempt to use Herman's office, though, as a sort of an appeal from your action?

Assistant Director De Costa:

We have a few who try to play one against the other.

Councilman Tuai:

Have you ever had a situation where a department head has refused to change something which is obviously wrong?

Mr. Loomis:

No sir, at least not since I've been on the job. If I don't get cooperation from the department head, I say, "Well, okay, can I arrange a time for you to explain to the Mayor why you are not going to do this?" That takes care of it.

Speaker Beppu:

Can I make an observation here? We have a very simple form of government, unlike other jurisdictions. We don't have local school boards, school districts, sanitary districts, or some other improvement districts. Yet, you have some confusion over state functions and county functions. I notice that Herman in a 10 month period had about 1500 calls; if that is so, as one of 51 House members, I should get roughly 20 to 30 calls which I haven't received. We come from a very small community, three quarters of a million

161

people, very congested, and we are very informal
as far as the relationship with our electorate is
concerned. We know our friends and neighbors, and we
know people from the other islands, yet we don't get
that many calls. Since we are very accessible,
I think it is very significant that the people would
call Herman's office or Jim's office instead.

Professor Wyner:
Is that the kind of situation that leads to some
jealousy on the part of legislators?

Speaker Beppu:
No, I don't think so. I'm very happy that they call
Jim and Herman, so they won't bug us.

Director Loomis:
To put it on a city level, we provide terrific
service for the Council.

Assistant Director De Costa:
We don't usurp any relationships that the Councilman
has with his constituents. We get the answer for
him, and if it satisfies him, then he'll call or
write to the complainant and say "This is the answer."
So, in effect, the elected official is being served
by our office. His image, if you will, is being
enhanced in the process.

Director Loomis:

It's my feeling that a very small percent of the
people who call our office with a complaint go away
unhappy. In most cases we are able to help them one way
or another. The very least we do for them is give them
a courteous, thoughtful, detailed explanation of
why we can't help them. In 99 percent of the cases
this is really all they are after. If they can't
get results, they at least want to know why, and
they want someone to take the time to explain it to
them. This, I think, prevents any significant
residual problems.

The University of Hawaii Ombudsman

Professor Moore:

I'd like to ask Charlie James, the University of Hawaii
Ombudsman, to discuss his relationship with Herman Doi's
office. There is overlap in both these cases, since Herman has
jurisdiction over the City and County as well as the
State University.

Ombudsman James:

I would like to mention how the office came about. It
was officially created by a resolution of the Board of
Regents last September, I believe. As such, it
doesn't have any basis in law, charters, or anything
like that. It's just part of the University organization.
Before it was set up, there was a good deal of comment

about where it ought to be. I believe that the
answer arrived at is the only one that's practical,
though it probably is not the best one. Actually,
I'm in the Executive Office of the President. I don't
think that it is too good an idea to have it this way,
but I will confess that even after six or seven
months on the job I don't know of any viable alternative
to it. It has to be some place, and that being the
case, I suppose this is about as good as any,
because the President doesn't bother /any, though I
might bother him a little bit once in a while. Probably
it doesn't make too much difference, because it depends
almost entirely on who it is and how he does it anyway.

The University, of course, is part of the State
government, and for those of you not from Hawaii I'd
like to stress that it is probably more intimately
part of the State government than what you are used
to elsewhere. The University budget is part of the
executive budget of the Governor. The University
is supported almost entirely by public funds, and
all the usual budgetary, personnel and other
controls apply in very large measure to the University,
as opposed to many state Universities you may be
used to which have a somewhat higher degree of autonomy.

The University is essentially a department of the
State government, although in my present capacity I
really have to argue with that--but it happens to be
a fact.

So, the question then is, what is it about the
University that would cause anybody to think they
need an Ombudsman when we already have one for the
State? I think it came up in several ways. In the
first place, it is fashionable these days. You know,
any self-respecting University has to have an
Ombudsman. It flows trippingly on the tongue, and
it's a nice thing to have. This has been building
up over quite a few years, I think. Some of you
guys have written up certain materials on this, and
it's got to be a hot idea. Another thing that
clearly had a great influence in our case was the last
three years, during which we had quite a series of
student demonstrations and a general feeling of student
need for a disinterested point of contact.

The existence of a state ombudsman office may have
helped to make this a familiar idea here, so that it
was more readily acceptable than would have otherwise been the case.

Ombudsman James:

A couple of days ago, I guess, John Moore had me on
the phone and he told me that I was supposed to talk
about how I worked with Herman Doi's office. I gave
him an answer then which is probably still true,
although Speaker Beppu has already upstaged me on it,
but I told him I gave Herman the tough ones and I
take the easy ones. People can--and people do--go
to both of us. We had two girls who had trouble
getting a refund on a trip to Europe. One of them
came to me one day, and the other went to see
Herman for assistance the next day. It took us a
couple of days to find out that we were working on
the same project. Then untangling it at the end to
be sure that everybody found out what had happened
was even more complicated. This, however, has been
rare.

We have a couple of rather consistent clients; one
of them keeps going to the Governor. She went to
Herman first, then to me, and she didn't get to
first base with either one of us. So now she has
taken to writing to the Governor all the time.

Actually, there have been a couple of cases that
have come to my attention where clearly some other
agency of the State government was involved. One of them
involved a boy in an apprentice program who was
complaining about the Department of Labor. Well, I
called up one of Herman's assistants and explained
the problem to him. I said, "Look you can handle
it a lot better than I can." He has taken it from
there.

There have been a couple of cases that came up through
the University to Herman's office and he gave them to
me. On others, we have retained a sort of a joint
interest; we have been operating largely on an exchange
of information, keeping each other up-to-date.

Operating Procedures
Ombudsman James:
Now, one thing that I did not recognize in Jim Loomis's
program was the overwhelming workload of 11,000.
I don't know how many phone calls I have got because I
don't register them. I've got about 110 recorded cases
since the first of November last year, some of which
are nothing, but at least two of which are still under
investigation, and it's probably going to take a good
part of the summer to try and make any sense out of
them--not the sort of thing you can deal with on the

167

phone.

Most of the work, however, is the sort of thing you can do over the phone. A great deal of it is people who just get lost. They walk into the business office or someplace and somebody turns them off and they don't know what to do. Some of them get into my office. Of course, this is the very small minority because the problems do apply to a lot of people. I'm speaking now of such things as getting hung up with registration, paying the wrong fees, getting your class schedule messed up and then getting it untangled again. These things apply to hundreds, perhaps thousands of students, of whom one or two or three might come in and see me.

I think this is fine, because it has so worked out that we haven't got much repeat business on these things. After getting one person's problem and following the thing through and getting it straightened out for him, it looks like--I can't prove this, but it looks like--other people don't encounter this problem any more. And I think this is probably the case in the more routine sorts of things.

Another thing that interests me in my short experience

is that the people you do the least for are the
most grateful. They fall all over themselves because
you were nice to them and explained something to them.
A good example of that was two girls who went down to
register for this semester. They got into line down
there, and then they discovered that their document
said they were supposed to register the next day, so
they wouldn't let them in. They said, "Well, we were
told we were supposed to register today." "Well,
the computer got fouled up. The computer put the wrong
day on here, you have to come back tomorrow." The
girls talked to me and I put them in touch with the
Dean of Students. It turned out that they had been
misinformed all along. In fact, they were scheduled to
register the next day, and once he sat down with
them and told them all this they were so happy they came
all the way back across campus to thank me for my very
great assistance, although they were in exactly the
same position when they walked out of my office as
they were when they walked in.

The other thing I was interested in was this
question of complaints and inquiries. We have had
a few cases that are real solid complaints, but we
don't call them that. There is no question that they
are. But because of the fact that most of them

probably fall into the category of inquiries, even
though they may have been stimulated by something that
looked fishy, we consider them to be inquiries.
Dissemination of information is one of the biggest
things that we do. The other things, the short-
cutting, getting to the guy that can do something for
them, is the other big volume thing. We do have eight
campuses to cover. Our total clientele, of course,
is minuscule compared to either of these other two
gentlemen. We have about 40,000 students in the
system as a whole, and I suppose maybe 10,000 faculty
and staff members. So, that gives us a total clientele
of 50,000, compared to three-quarters of a million.

This may not look very good, but it takes relatively
more time because we cover each campus once a month.
We also have been stopping in there at night to
catch the night students because these folks get
left out completely. They are step-children of step-
children. Some of these kids were delighted to have
someone come round and talk to them, although they
didn't have much to say. The apprenticeship problems
would never have come to light if we hadn't been
scurrying around these community colleges at night.

Workload outside of the main campus is very light

in terms of the number of cases. There are not very

many. Maybe the main thing that we do at these

other campuses, rather than solve problems and

investigate cases, is to glue the University system

together. There isn't anybody else in the University

system who makes a point of going around and sitting

down with these folks, drinking coffee--which may

sound pretty worthless considering how much money

I make, but the fact is that to the extent that there

is a need for this kind of glue in the system as a

whole, we provide it. It's not complaint work; it's

probably not Ombudsman work.

The question of money has been raised a couple of times

today. Again, my situation is quite different from

the other two gentlemen. Largely, because it isn't set

up on a legal basis, I suppose. Funding this year

came from the Division of Business Affairs at the

University where I previously worked; they lopped off

$45,000 for the Ombudsman office. I'm not going to

spend all that this year.

We don't intend to set up a position of Ombudsman at

the University as such, because if you did you would

get tangled up in the salary situation. When I went into this job I just took my previous salary with me. When I go out, and I may not survive the first year, it is possible that an assistant professor might get this assignment. He would move over into that job and he could take his salary with him.

Professor Moore:
One thing I particularly noted was that you have received 110 inquiries--some more substantial than others--since you have been there. I expect that is a much larger volume than Herman was receiving from the University before you were appointed which suggests that your presence at the campus generates an additional number of complaints, and perhaps that there is somewhat greater flexibility to your role. That is, I gather that you are able to do things that Herman probably would not be able to do, given the specifications of his job.

Ombudsman James:
I think in many of these cases it's easier for me to do these things. I think all of these things could be done through Herman's office, but in the first place it's a lot of clutter and nonsense for him, say, if someone gets in the wrong registration line. It's much easier for me being right there to clear up

these little things as they go along. This does not
apply to major things, which could just as well be
performed by Herman's office as by mine.

Professor Moore:
So, it's not just a question of decentralizing Herman's
office. You really have a somewhat different kind
of function, which supports or adds to the
Ombudsmanic function.

Mr. Kaye:
What is the jurisdiction of your office?

Ombudsman James:
The definition, the best I can remember it, is to
make sure the students are given proper attention
and to advise on University policies and procedures.
This fuzzy, funny kind of language really comes
from the fact that there was quite a question as to
whether I ought to cover faculty matters, and
things like that, or whether it was just students.
It mentions students, but it does not say I can't
do the other thing.

I have been handling quite a few minor faculty
problems. Now, I've told everybody I'm not going
to get into tenure problems, I'm not going to get into
the problems where a guy gets canned, except perhaps

to see that he gets whatever process is due him.
But in terms of the result or advocacy or anything like
that, I won't do it.

Mr. Kaye:
Well how about, say student-faculty or student-
administration type of thing?

Ombudsman James:
That's the main part. Most of it is students who
come in and have got a beef against a faculty member,
a beef against the business office. I suppose about
40% of my job is probably involved in business affairs,
about 40% in student affairs and maybe 20% in the
academic area. Some of the more rewarding ones and
the more interesting ones, have come out of the
academic area.

I got a very solid complaint that one of our schools
was really abusing its students. Although I had
always heard that this school was not a very good
place, and even though all this beefing and complaining had been going around, nobody had even talked
to the Dean until I went down there with a kind of bill
of particulars one day and said, "now look, let's talk
about this." He had heard these rumors, but no one
had ever sat down and told him what the problem was.

Although all is not sweetness and light in that
school now, I am sure that it has improved a good deal.

There is one big group of employees for which I am the
only recourse--that's the student employee. There is
no civil service law for them, no faculty tenure
policies. They work there at sufferance, and
there isn't even much in the way of rules involved.
I've got quite a lot of these, most of them having
to do with pay, some with working conditions.
There must be more, because I haven't had a single
person come in and complain about these things that
hasn't been justified yet.

Mr. Kaye:
Have you turned away any complaints for lack of
jurisdiction yet?

Ombudsman James:
We tell people we'll be glad to talk with them. If
there is nothing I can do for them, I'll tell them
there is nothing I can do for them. I can't really
think of a case, however, when I've just said "well,
look, this isn't my business." I've got one coming up
next Monday--a woman is coming in about a tenure
question. I got it actually from an attorney here
in town. I told him that I wasn't sure I could do

175

anything for her, but I would be glad to talk to her.

Speaker Beppu:
I've got a question, Charlie. I don't know what it would do to the office University-wide, since it is the only state university here. What if the University Ombudsman came under Herman's office? Would it enhance the office? Would it be strengthened or weakened?

Ombudsman James:
It would strengthen it in terms of muscle, but I think it might weaken it in terms of what the people think the University Ombudsman's job ought to be. There is no question it would improve the status of the office. Whether it would improve the effectiveness of it, or hurt the effectiveness of it, in dealing particularly with the student body, I have some reservations about that. I only have to guess. I think maybe it would hurt a little bit.

Speaker Beppu:
I have some reservations about the students and the faculty thinking that they are so separate from the state government or the rest of the population that this should be a specialized office.

Ombudsman Doi:
I think the way it is now serves a valuable purpose

in the sense of providing immediate service on campus.
The way we are operating presently, if a student is
not satisfied he can still come to us. It provides him
with two means of access.

Summary

Impact of Ombudsman Offices on Related Grievance Mechanisms
  Professor Anderson:
One of the questions raised by the Ombudsman-designate
in Seattle was whether, after he had been going for a
while, he could make some very broadgauged suggestions
for administrative reform. I recall that Herman Doi
said that the main thing is to get your own office
established, and not to be that ambitious, but he
didn't preclude it as a possibility later on.

I'd like to comment on that, and tie it in with what
has been going on here. I know of no Ombudsman office
that has been successful in becoming a Little Hoover
Commission, making widespread recommendations for
overhaul of an administrative system. We can see from
Herman Doi's suggestions for legislative reform that
they tend to be of an order that is specific,
relating to specific problems. Generally, then, that
is a modest contribution compared to other ones
that he has listed as part of his office. He is not a

one-man walking constitutional convention.

But, I think there is one exception to that, and
that is in the area of grievance mechanisms per se.
It is here that the Ombudsman seems to make a direct
contribution to the organization of government.

One of the things you do when you set up an
Ombudsman office is to take an inventory of pre-
existing grievance mechanisms. Ultimately, when
there is a weakness somewhere in grievance machinery,
the Ombudsman is going to know about it because
that is where he gets a volume of business. I'm
just suggesting at this point that if there hadn't
been a Honolulu Office of Information and Complaint,
one would have had to be created or else he would have
just been overwhelmed, given the kind of office that
his is supposed to be.

Ombudsman Doi:
I would have died if I had gotten all those complaints.

Professor Moore:
Pursuing this point, Jim, have you found that your
office has produced a similar kind of result in
terms of upgrading the procedures in the agencies
that you work with? Have they improved their own
mechanisms?

178

Director Loomis:

I think there is no question about it. There are
numerous examples. The first one that comes to mind
was an incident a month or so ago when a
traffic accident took City and County ambulances an
hour and fifteen minutes to get there, through an
incredible series of foul-ups and coincidence. As
a result, we instituted a sort of a fail-safe system
in the dispatching of the ambulances. There are
many, many examples.

Ombudsman Walton:

Did you initiate this solution?

Director Loomis:

Yes. It was a very complicated thing involving the
similarity of Hawaiian names and everything else.
It took us a whole lot longer to find out what
happened than it did to suggest a solution.

Assistant Director De Costa:

We have helped the various departments, such as the
Planning Department, to create avenues by which people
can present their views directly to the department.
Right now, I have been working for several months with
the Planning Department revising a questionnaire that
they will distribute. Actually it's something people
either can sign or hand in anonymously, that they
will get right at the counter of the Planning Department.

179

My feeling is that after a few weeks the Planning
Department will find out just what people think about
them.

  Professor Moore:
As you will note from the agenda, we are going to
have some people here this afternoon from the
administrative agencies, so we will be able to ask
them directly how they feel about all these ombudsmanic
services. But I wondered if each of you could compare
notes for us on your own perception of the reaction
of agency people to your activities. Does it annoy
them? Do they think it is a help? How do you
read their response?

  Director Loomis:
I would say it varies from individual to individual,
really. I hope that all of these people realize,
as I said earlier, that when I call, or when Pat calls,
it's just like the Mayor is calling. I hope they
have that one essential idea.

  Professor Moore:
You want them to feel slightly threatened?

  Director Loomis:
Yes. I don't think it's necessary in the vast majority
of cases, but some of these people are pretty fat.
They have been in the civil service for a long time,

within one department, and they get a little callous. I think in these cases, which perhaps are few and far between, you have to have that clout. As to their attitude, or the way they respond, this is an individual thing.

Assistant Director De Costa:
Very often the City is right, rather than the complainant. Having an objective third party, such as the Miss Fix-It or Kokua Line complaint columns, explain in their own language how the City is right actually exonerates and explains the position of the city department or employee. If you read the columns closely you will find that very often inquiries and complaints are based on misinformation or misconceptions. When these are cleared up, it actually does the department a service.

Ombudsman James:
There are two additional considerations in the reaction of the University to my office. One was that I'd been there for quite a few years myself, and I knew most of the people. The other was that a great number of people think what they do is their own business and nobody else's. "What's all this? Nobody ever asked me this question before." Maybe the proof of this was the school I was talking about where the Dean

had been under serious fire, but never under direct fire. Everybody had been complaining about it over a martini or something. In fact, I found one report of six or seven pages written by an Assistant Vice President which had been filed in the Vice President's office and never even shown to this guy. He was a little bit shook up when I first went to see him. I got him a copy of the report. It had been lying around all these months and he hadn't even known of its existence. In a little while I think he came pretty much the full circle, and understanding the issues better, took constructive action.

I also subscribe to the idea that it doesn't hurt to scare people just a little bit.

Professor Moore:
If I can summarize what we have so far in the way of contributions to agency personnel: (1) You can exonerate them publicly in a way that helps to make clear that they were not at fault; and (2) You can draw to their attention grievances that have just been circulating around, but never brought to them in a way that could be acted upon.

Speaker Beppu:
We have heard "muscle" and "clout" used. I think Herman

carries a lot of muscle in his office with regard
to the State departments. They know his office
represents 76 legislators, 25 in the Senate, 51
in the House. I think this is very important, that
department heads who are appointed by the Governor
and confirmed by the Senate will move when Herman's
office calls them, and even in the county governments,
because our statute with regard to this office
provides that Herman can move into the county area.
He can ask for information; he can ask for the
records.

Professor Moore:
That's an interesting point, because I think we tend
to assume generally that muscle or clout comes from
executive offices--from mayors, or perhaps from the
President's office at the University--and overlook
the fact that an Ombudsman office that is established
by the Legislature and that enjoys the continuing
support of the Legislature has some clout, too.

Speaker Beppu:
Herman can move in, too, in regard to private or
quasi-public agencies, where public funds are
appropriated.

Ombudsman Doi:
For example, the Legal Aid Society and the Public

Defender. A case involving these agencies is not
really treated as a complaint under which we have
definite jurisdiction, but we have been able to make
contact with them and get answers from them with regard
to specific complaints. They have been more than
willing to help, because they know the funding comes
from the Legislature.

The Hawaii Medical Services Association is another
example. Since the State has a large contract with
this organization for health and medical benefits, we
have been able to query them about certain kinds of
things.

Professor Anderson:
What about complaints about private parties, professionals who are licensed by the state, where the
accusation if valid might lead one to question whether
the licensing function was being properly exercised--
including subsequent supervision of people who are
licensed? Do you ever get any of these?

Ombudsman Doi:
Oh yes, we have had a number of cases involving the
commissions and boards that license people in the
State. Many private complaints we refer to the
boards, and we monitor the board's decisions in
regard to those specific complaints. In that sense,

there is a kind of indirect relationship to private
transactions.

Assistant Director De Costa:
Another example at the city level involves safety
inspection stations. Rather than having our own,
we have authorized certain service stations throughout
the island. When we get complaints and they are
justified after investigation, the first procedure is
to suspend the station. Usually, on the second
complaint that station is discontinued, unless
there is a very good reason. This is being done
under the auspices of the City and County government.
These are service stations that have the authority
from the City Council to either approve or deny
safety inspection stickers for $3.25, and many of
them don't even put the car on the rack. Others will
put it on the rack and they will find a lot of things
that will lead to a $100 job for them. We have
investigated a lot of these complaints together with
the Police Department and have taken action against
a lot of stations. Usually, after that, they toe the
line.

Ombudsman Doi:
Private towing companies are another example, because
of the contract relationship between the City and the
tow companies.

Assistant Director De Costa:
We have new contracts coming up now, and Clarence
Maki and I have sent a detailed memo to the
Finance Director with complaints we have received and
recommendations of things that should be written into
the new contracts. This is one that seems very small,
and yet it is very large. They are agents of the
City, but we have no way of directly requiring the
same level of service and courtesy as we do of our
own city employees. Very often people call and say,
"gee, you're supposed to have my car," but they
say, "I'm busy, come back later, wait a while,"
and the guy has to wait two hours to get his car
back. We have categorized all these complaints,
and have asked the Finance Director to write appropriate
provisions into the new contracts, so that we can
require more service of the towing contractors.

Director Loomis:
Another point that goes back to how the departments
react to us. I think in many cases we can take a lot
of heat off these departments--serve as a sort of
buffer between the departments and the public. We
can forestall, put off, explain in advance, or
whatever you want to call it, complaints which
would otherwise occupy members of their staff.

The next point was about the way we deal with departments, agencies, over which we have no control. For example, a fellow called me a week or so ago and complained that the air conditioner on the roof of a commercial building, just below his window, was very noisy. There are all kinds of ways we can legally go about making it quieter. First of all, it's under State jurisdiction, they could send someone out with a meter to take the decibel readings and all that. In this case, I called the manager of that building and told him who I was, where I was calling from, that we had received a complaint and could we get his cooperation. Absolutely no problem. He had some people up there working on the equipment.

Assistant Director De Costa:
Yes, we deal as human beings. We had a case of an old building that is going to be torn down because a manufacturer has bought the land and is going to construct a factory there. The people who own the company are good people. They don't want to throw the tenants out. They have a lot of welfare clients living there. But the deadline that they gave them seemed too short. So, by talking to the owners on the telephone, on a human, person-to-person basis, we got their okay to extend the deadline for the reloca-

187

tion of the people who now occupy the old boarding
house, and should we not be able to reach that
deadline, they will extend it. This means that
their financing will cost them more, because they
then have to delay construction another two weeks,
another month. But then we got the Welfare Department
to cooperate, and I think we have relocated almost
all of them now. We only have a few left. The
deadline extension has really helped out,
because otherwise these people would have been out on
the street in the month of May, or as they said,
they were going to come into our office and sleep.

Professor Moore:
I note two things in your comments. First, how
personalized these activities are, which is one of
the benefits which is supposed to attach to an
Ombudsmanic function. Secondly, how permeable the
jurisdictional lines are.

Director Loomis:
Half the time, this is why they are here anyway,
because they have run into arbitary boundaries
and red tape and are fed up.

Professor Moore:
Well, continuing my list of benefits to the agencies,
it now includes exonerate, alert and buffer. I wonder,
Herman, if you could reinforce or perhaps extend that

188

list?

Assistant Director De Costa:
This is one advantage we have of being an office
of information and complaint--if we have been too hard
on a department, then we do a nice story to show
some worthwhile thing they are doing.

Ombudsman Doi:
I have to agree with Jim that it differs from
person to person. Each department has its own view
of what our operations are like, and what effect it
has on its own security. Some of them definitely feel
that it does point out areas of weakness in their
own administration, which they are interested in
learning about and in buttressing to be sure that
they are providing efficient service. In that sense,
it helps them in identifying problem areas within their
jurisdictions.

In others, you get a sort of negative response.
Perhaps the feeling may be different as you go down
the ladder. On the lower level, the employees may
feel that here is another person looking over their
shoulder, checking on what they are doing, and they
feel jeopardized. As you go up the scale, perhaps
the feeling is lessened because they have a much

broader view of the problem.

Director Loomis:
It all boils down to how conscientious the guy
is about his job.

Ombudsman Doi:
If he is really there to do a job, to improve the
efficiency of his department, he'll look at it
positively and see that it does help him to identify
administrative weaknessess.

"The More You Do, The More You Get"
Assistant Director De Costa:
There is one point I wanted to make to other jurisdictions that are thinking about setting up complaint
procedures or grievance procedures, Ombudsmanlike
functions. You are not thereby going to eradicate
complaints, or cut them down.

The more you do, the more complaints you generate.
A good example is the new City bus service. We have
had more people call or come into our office and say
that they are so happy that the Mayor has put the bus
service in, that "It's amazing how he and the
councilmen were able to do it--but, the door is in the
back." So we got all these complaints and we went down,
and we spent the whole morning at the yard. We

190

crawled in and out of the buses, we went through
their files, their lists of complaints and how
they handled them, and everything. We were able to
come up with some suggestions for improvement in the
service and their relationships with the public.

Director Loomis:
On the same subject of the buses, under the old
system of private operation, these drivers never
had any training in terms of courtesy, or public
relations. The same drivers are now driving the
City buses, and as it became apparent that we
were going to have a public relations problem, as
the complaints came in from private citizens about
the few drivers that were discourteous, the net
result was that we instituted a training program
for these drivers. Some of them have been driving
buses in Honolulu for 20 years, and they are just
now getting into a training program that in part
will emphasize courtesy.

Assistant Director De Costa:
And this was recommended by one of our staff members.

Professor Anderson:
But then you can reduce the complaints. You say they
increase because you get into an activity like that,
but then hopefully you can decrease them.

Director Loomis:
No, no. Because before, you see, people didn't
bother to complain.

Mr. James:
You don't ever complain about something that doesn't
exist. I was a little instrumental in extending
some of the library hours on some of the outlying
campuses. No one was complaining about the book
collection or the staff or anything, because the place
was closed up all the time. As soon as you get
them open so that somebody can use them, right away
all of the frailties of the system expose themselves.

Assistant Director De Costa:
If you didn't do something about complaints, people
wouldn't bother complaining. You make the office
what you want to make it.

RELATIONSHIPS WITH RESPONDENT AGENCIES
Professor Moore:
I would like to introduce some new guests to the
conference: Deputy Chief Charles Duarte of the
Honolulu Police Department, and Director Ralph W.
Kondo of the State Department of Taxation.

Just to bring you two up-to-date, we have put
Herman Doi through his paces in describing his
office, his procedures, and his view of the

Ombudsmanic function. We have tried to put that
function in context by comparing it with other
related services, such as that provided by the
office of Information and Complaint, the role
played by legislators in handling their casework,
and the similar function performed by the new
Ombudsman for the University of Hawaii.

This afternoon, we would like to get the perspective
of agency personnel on the function performed by the
Ombudsman office. We are confident that candor
will not be inhibited by Herman Doi's presence.
If I could just ask you, then, to describe briefly
the nature of your contact with the Ombudsman office,
what appears to be the utility of the office from
your standpoint, and then the potential cost it
may pose to your own office.

Professor Anderson:
And perhaps describe the mechanisms for complaint within your department.

Professor Moore:
Yes, and that as well. It's important in both cases.
I know in the case of the Police Department there is
a very elaborate procedure for reviewing and evaluating
complaints, and I know there is an open door policy

in the Taxation Department for dealing with
complaints from the public. Can we start with you,
Director Kondo?

The State Department of Taxation
Director Kondo:
Since we are the Department of Taxation, naturally
our contact with the Ombudsman has been with reference
to taxpayers and their problems. As you have
already stated, we do have an open door policy. We
regard every complaint that comes to us as a matter
of importance. The fact that a complaint might come
from the Ombudsman's Office is not given any particular
significance. By that, I mean we treat every taxpayer alike. That's our policy.

However, I think the existence of the Ombudsman's
Office does serve a very important purpose. It does
assist us by calling to our attention the existence
of some possibly inequitable practices. Because
of the extent of our services, we are not
always correct, that's for sure. We welcome criticism
from anyone in all of our operations. Of course, we
treat all complaints seriously, and we attempt to
correct all errors on our part. Basically, we are
very concerned about inequities. We want to make
sure that all taxpayers under similar circumstances are

194

treated alike. This is one of my basic concerns.
This is why I welcome the creation and existence
of the Ombudsman's office.

Professor Moore:
What about procedural matters? Have there been
any cases where it's not so much a question of equity--
that is, one person being treated differently from
another person--but rather a way of improving a
whole category of services or actions?

Director Kondo:
Well, I've found that our people are government-
oriented, and tax-administration oriented. They feel
that their goal is to collect taxes, period. That
is not my policy. Because of their feeling about
that, their attitude toward taxpayers I guess
is a little bit...how shall I say it?

Professor Anderson:
...high handed?

Director Kondo:
Well not quite high handed, but...

Professor Moore:
Not exactly accommodating?

Director Kondo:
Well, that's true. Although this attitude is changing,
possibly because our policy has been to answer all
complaints.

Professor Moore:
At what level would a complaint enter your office?

Director Kondo:
Well, we have no particular procedure set up at
the present time, but the complaint usually comes
through the lowest level person. Then, if the
complainant is not happy, he is referred to the
supervisor, then to the administrator, and from
him possibly to me.

Professor Moore:
So a complaint could go through as many as four
levels.

Director Kondo:
Also, complaints go to the Governor, and then
he can refer the complaint to us, or to legislators,
who then refer the case to us, and naturally to the
Ombudsman.

Professor Moore:
Do you ever refer any complainants to the
Ombudsman after they have come to you, if they are
still unhappy?

Director Kondo:
I believe we have on very few occasions.

Professor Moore:
What is your reading of the reaction of your staff
to the presence of the Ombudsman?

Director Kondo:

I would say the first reaction, and a natural one
I guess, is one of irritation, being told to explain
our actions and what we have done as far as taxpayers
are concerned. But I think that feeling is gradually
going away. We accept the fact that there is an
Ombudsman, and that we make errors and that we are
sometimes inconsistent. We certainly have to
correct our practices.

Professor Anderson:

The Ombudsman supports your office, too, on some of
these complaints?

Director Kondo:

Oh yes, he does.

Ombudsman Walton:

Did you know Herman before he was selected for the
position?

Director Kondo:

Yes.

Ombudsman Walton:

In terms of apprehension within the Department, in
retrospect, is there anything Herman might have
done to ameliorate that condition at the beginning?

Director Kondo:

I think Herman has been very concerned about the
relationship between various agencies and his office.

He came to my office.

Ombudsman Walton:
Did this help? Was it beneficial?

Director Kondo:
I think so. I think my staff began to realize the
reason for the existence of such an office.

Professor Moore:
We have mentioned both some benefits and some
costs. Among the benefits there is the identification
of a problem that you might not have recognized
otherwise, and the perhaps occasional exoneration or
explanation to the complainant of the correctness of
your action. Then, you mentioned one possible
cost, that initial sense of irritation. Are there
any additional benefits or costs that you perceive?
Is it burdensome, for example, to respond to
inquiries from the Ombudsman?

Director Kondo:
Yes, it is burdensome to us, although we now accept
this as part of our function, to reply to the
Ombudsmanic requests.

Professor Moore:
Did you have to expand your conception of your
responsibilities to include this?

Director Kondo:
As far as we are concerned, we didn't find it too

difficult to accept the existence of the Ombudsman's
office, because in fact we have been doing this
ourselves. The burden to us, primarily, is in the
area of our having to investigate the nature of the
complaint to determine the facts and finally to
prepare the report. That is a very burdensome task
for us.

Councilman Tuai:
Do you do that regardless of where the complaint
comes from?

Director Kondo:
Not necessarily. We can call the taxpayer in
and have a conference on a verbal basis. This is
much easier than writing a written report.

Professor Anderson:
Do you think there is any difference in the kinds
of cases that come to you by way of the Ombudsman that
makes it appropriate to have this more cumbersome way
of handling them, or are the kinds of things you
get from the Ombudsman's office pretty much the same
kind you get directly from the Governor or a legislator?

Director Kondo:
No, I haven't been able to discover any kind of pattern.
However, I must say that the Ombudsman's office is
very persistent.

Ombudsman Walton:
Do most of the complaints you receive deal with the conduct of your employees, or do they deal with technicalities of the tax laws?

Director Kondo:
I would say most deal with technicalities in tax laws or with our interpretations. I'd say complaints about our people and their attitude are very very few in number.

Professor Anderson:
John Moore listed irritation as a cost rather than a reward, but I wonder if there isn't a potentially beneficial aspect to that sense of irritation. Let me put it as a question, Director Kondo: Do you think that sense of irritation might cause your people to be more careful, and if so, is that carefulness itself an asset, or does it perhaps go too far to the other extreme, so that they could become hypercautious?

Director Kondo:
I think I prefaced my remark about being irritated, by saying it's a natural reaction.

Professor Anderson:
Does it persist and actually change the mental set of your workers, so that they might just be a little bit more careful?

Director Kondo:
Well, I certainly hope this is a result.

Councilman Tuai:
How many complaints do you have per year?

Director Kondo:
I really don't know the answer to that. Right now
we have a newly created, or temporarily created,
Office of Complaints, and I think it was created
in January, or earlier this year. Mostly, they
get inquiries.

Professor Moore:
What brought about the establishment of a Complaint
Office in your Department?

Director Kondo:
Well, dealing with my people gave me the impression
that they were more interested in collecting taxes
than in educating the public as to the requirements
of the tax laws. So, I took it upon myself to adopt
the policy that the most important thing as far as
our Department was concerned is to educate the
taxpayer with their responsibility to pay taxes.

Professor Moore:
This morning when the HOIC people were here, they
pointed out how important it was for the effectiveness
of their office to have the support of the Mayor, how
absolutely essential it was. If the Mayor did not
have an interest in providing this service it would

be essentially a dead letter, because there is not sufficient provision in the City Charter to assure its vitality. I think something parallel to this certainly applies at the state level, and I thought, Mr. Kondo, you might just elaborate a little bit on the Governor's attitude and his instructions to his cabinet.

Director Kondo:
Well, in my view the Ombudsman's Office has been a success, one of the principal reasons for this being that the Governor has issued a directive to all the directors of the various departments to cooperate in full with the Ombudsman. As you stated, without this cooperation there would be no Ombudsman's Office. Of course, the fact that we are all appointed by him is very important. The question that comes to my mind is, supposing we had all been elected, whether or not we would be as cooperative as we are now. I've thought about this, and I think we would still be cooperative, partly because we would want to be reelected. It is very important to keep the electorate happy.

Ombudsman Walton:
Assuming his method of operation was to use the press to publicize his activities, would you still have the same basic feeling?

Director Kondo:
I think I would be more resentful.

Professor Moore:
Let me put this question to you. Assuming that
there is a need to publicize the Ombudsman's services
so that people have a real opportunity to take advantage
of them, but recognizing the possibility of greater
resentment stemming from that publicity can you
think of ways in which the Ombudsman might be able
to more widely publicize his services without causing
that kind of resentment?

Director Kondo:
Well, as far as I am concerned if Herman desires to
publicize the existence of the services of his
office I have no objection to that. That's entirely
his prerogative, so long as there is no reference
to the Department of Taxation.

Professor Moore:
What would you think about a summary of a case that
he cited as an example of his services?

Director Kondo:
That's no problem, as long as no direct reference
is made. I don't think it is fair to any department
to have a direct reference made.

Ombudsman Walton:
There are references to departments in his annual
reports. Has that offended you?

Director Kondo:

No. I guess we assume that annual reports must

be prepared. But when it is for the newspapers,

that is something else again.

The Honolulu Police Department

Professor Moore:

Chief Duarte, could you begin with a brief description

of complaint-handling procedures within the Police

Department, and perhaps a characterization of the

types of complaints that you receive, and then

proceed to link your procedures with the Ombudsman's

Office?

Chief Duarte:

We have always had an Inspection Section to investigate

all complaints. We have approximately one inspector

and three lieutenants assigned to that particular

section. Prior to July 1, 1969, the date of

the inception of the Ombudsman's Office, most of

our complaints, of course, were made directly to

the Police Department, and also through the

Office of Information and Complaint in the Mayor's

office. After July 1, 1969, we just followed

the same procedures.

Our relationship has always been very good, from the

very outset. We were quite apprehensive in the

beginning, but I think that was dispelled after

our meeting with Mr. Doi. He was quite candid about the whole thing, and he was critical of certain aspects of our investigations and asked if they could sit in on investigations. As I said, we were quite apprehensive, but we acceded to their request.

According to our statistics, they sat in on exactly six of our interviews and during some of the interrogations and interviews they participated actively. They questioned witnessess, and they questioned the accused officer. I think the total number of complaints we have received was sixteen, that went directly to the inspector's office, since the inception of the Ombudsman. Several other procedural complaints were directed to the divisions concerned, like the Traffic Division and tow services. These were resolved with members of his staff verbally.

But, really, it has been a very amicable relationship, and I say that in all candor. I don't care whether Mr. Doi is here or not. This is a fact. That in essence is the situation. Of course, I think our investigations are quite comprehensive, and they have always been rather comprehensive, sometimes too comprehensive.

Professor Moore:

Have you found increased demands placed on your
staff as a result of the Ombudsman's involvement?

Chief Duarte:

Oh, yes. We have asked for additional personnel,
additional lieutenants, so that will help us considerably. As I've said, we had 16 complaints, cases
that we responded to, have had to investigate.
But, there were quite a few others that were
directed to the various divisions, so it did
involve some additional work.

Professor Moore:

Can I impose on you to describe the process that
you normally employ? I have the feeling that
some people might think that 16 complaints from
the Ombudsman's office over a period of nearly two
years is not really a whole lot of complaints, but
I know, having talked to you before, how
extensive your investigations are.

Chief Duarte:

Initially, if I recall correctly, conduct—complaints
against police officers were recorded at the Ombudsman
office and he forwarded the reports to the Police
Department, and we would investigate the complaint.
At the conclusion of the investigation we would
send the reports back to the Ombudsman's office,
where one of the men there would review the reports.

The copies of all the arrest reports were forwarded to his office for review. If he found something was deficient he would call it to our attention. We had very little difficulty there as I recall.

After that, as I understand it, when the complainant would go to his office they would sign a complaint, and if the complainant refused to sign the form, or was reluctant to cooperate, the complaint would be withdrawn. This way we were able to weed out some of the chronic complainants.

Presently, they are working out a new policy and attempting to resolve most of the complaints and also the difficulties, I guess, in the Office of the Ombudsman. If they can't resolve it there, then they refer it to us. This is the procedure we have followed. We haven't experienced any real difficulty.

Professor Moore:
So there has been some shift, then, in the burden of investigation?

Chief Duarte:
Yes.

Ombudsman Doi:
I think what we are doing that is different from
the beginning is we have been doing some
investigation on our own, besides relying purely on
the police reports themselves. I think this is
because we have some staff now, whereas when we
first started we didn't. We just took the allegations down and shot them over to his office. Some
very invalid complaints might require extensive
investigation which would waste their time.

Chief Duarte:
They are screening many of the cases.

Professor Moore:
Do you regard that as helpful?

Chief Duarte:
Very progressive.

Ombudsman Walton:
With reference to signing a complaint, do you ask
a citizen to sign a complaint in your office?

Ombudsman Doi:
We have a new policy. If it is a specific complaint
against a specific employee making all kinds of
allegations about what has transpired, we request
he sign something stating what those allegations are.

Ombudsman Walton:
Is that true of all departments?

Ombudsman Doi:
All departments.

Councilman Tuai:
Are they taken under oath?

Ombudsman Doi:
No. We require the signature. You find people are
very reluctant to sign something if they know it
isn't exactly correct. They take great care to put
it in the form that is most truthful.

Chief Duarte:
You might say that one thing that helped us was the
sitting in on our investigations. I think that this
established a very good relationship.

Professor Moore:
How did the police officers who were involved feel
about this?

Chief Duarte:
Rather apprehensive, certainly. But after a while,
I think they were rather settled and they knew this
was a necessity.

Ombudsman Doi:
The other aspect we ran across is that the unions
that represented the police officers were quite
concerned about our respecting the rights of the
officers themselves. We sat down with them and told
them that as far as we were concerned, we were
willing to go through a warning system--warning him

of his constitutional rights, and if he wants to
bring along his union representative, fine, bring
him in. So that allayed the fears of the union,
and I think to some extent it allayed the fears
of the officers themselves.

Professor Moore:
Were such representatives ever brought in?

Ombudsman Doi:
Not to my knowledge. We have interviewed officers,
but they have been more than willing to state their
position, what happened and all the rest of it without any reluctance, although they were told that if
they did not wish to testify this was fine with us.

Chief Duarte:
We haven't had that difficulty.

Professor Wyner:
I was wondering, Chief, about any differences that
officers might feel with so called internal grievance
mechanisms--that is, a complaint that originates
with you, and stays within the Department--compared
to a case in which the Ombudsman is involved.
Do your officers have any preference? If you have to
be accused, is it better to be accused through one
system than another?

Chief Duarte:

I don't think so. We have not had this experience.
I think initially, as I said, because members of
the Ombudsman staff would sit in on the investigation,
naturally there was concern at the outset, but this was
dispelled after two or three of these investigations.

Professor Moore:

There was no organized opposition to the Ombudsman
office on grounds that it would become a kind of
civilian police review board?

Chief Duarte:

No. If there was any such feeling, it rested with
the Chief and myself. And I think we expressed this
to Mr. Doi. We tried to be very-candid. But,
personally, I'm very pleased with the way it turned
out. We more than welcomed the assistance,
because some of the procedural things helped us considerably, I think.

I can recall one complaint on the towing situation.
We'd all go down to the Ombudsman's office and they
would have laid out on the blackboard exactly what
our procedures were, and then would recommend ways in
which we could improve these procedures. It seems
that we would be confronted with these things every
day, that we would be able to resolve them.
But, you know, when you are so close to the thing you

can't see it. They were able to do this more object-
ively, and they really helped us. Again, I'm not
being nice. It's just a matter of fact.

Professor Moore:
Do you think that complainants feel a little more
reassured after the correctness of the Police
Department's action has been explained to them by
the Ombudsman?

Chief Duarte:
This is one result of the Ombudsman's office that
has been a good thing. We opened it up to public
scrutiny, and I think this breeds trust and confidence which I thought we had in the beginning,
but not to the extent we have it now. I think
that the public has supported us all the way.

Professor Wyner:
Has there been any increase or decrease or no change,
say, in the last couple of years since the institution
of the Ombudsman office?

Chief Duarte:
I'm sure that we have these figures, but I don't have
them with me. I would say that there has been an
increase in the number of complaints. I think people
have felt at ease. Probably they were a little
apprehensive to come to the Police Department directly,
but with the Ombudsman's office and the Office of

Information and Complaint at the Mayor's office,
I think they feel a little freer, more at ease and so
on.

Naturally, this generated more complaints, more
work for us, and consequently at one stage we had
one lieutenant and one inspector in the office,
now we have two lieutenants and we are asking for
one additional because these reports do take
two or three months to complete, and this had been
a cause for concern not only to us but to the Ombudsman's office. We are trying to rectify that now.

Ombudsman Walton:
In cases of complaints that start originally with
your Department, have you ever encountered a situation
where they then appeal your decision to Herman's
office? Or, have you reached an impasse and then
referred them to his office as an outside arbitrator?

Chief Duarte:
I don't know. Can you recall anything like that,
Herman?

Ombudsman Doi:
No. We have had a situation where they complained
to both.

Mr. Douglas:
What percent of the complaints were valid?

Chief Duarte:
Out of sixteen cases, one allegation was sustained.
In all of the rest, there was not sufficient
evidence or some question remained.

Mr. Douglas:
Mr. Doi, are you satisfied with that record?

Ombudsman Doi:
Well, we received all the files and conducted our
own interviews and we were satisfied that the
investigations were accurate. In most cases
where you have a one-to-one confrontation, you
really cannot tell who is telling you the truth.
In that situation, you cannot recommend punishment
of the officer if you have no tangible proof.

Chief Duarte:
The officers have been a lot more careful about
that. If something happens, they are told to get
witnesses as soon as they can, even before resolving
anything.

Ombudsman Walton:
What was the reaction of the other fifteen?

Ombudsman Doi:
We never heard from them.

The policy that we have is that we will not turn
over the police report to the complainant or to his
attorney or to anyone else. The complainant himself
may come in and read the report in our office.
However, we do provide him with a written answer
in that we will summarize what is contained in the
police report and make it available to him,
explaining the reasons and the basis of our opinion.

Professor Moore:
What percentage of complaints are routed to your
office through the Mayor's Office of Information
and Complaint?

Chief Duarte:
About the same.

Professor Moore:
Sometimes those are jointly pursued, are they not?

Ombudsman Doi:
Yes.

We have had occasion to have both. In fact, when we
were talking to the officer, the person in charge of
the City Office of Information & Complaint
was physically there with my analyst and also
asking questions, so that in one investigation we satisfied the Police Department, our office and the city
office.

Chief Duarte:

Yes, and another thing, usually when we dispose of
a case, the case is reviewed by the Corporation
Counsel and he also will render his decision or
recommendations. If he is in accord, then it will
be so specified.

Professor Moore:

Do any of them carry up to the Board of Police
Commissioners?

Chief Duarte:

Not yet.

Professor Wyner:

I wonder if I could ask a question about some of
your training procedures for police officers. I know
Mr. Doi has talked to some cadets or trainees.
Is that the primary training they receive in the kinds
of complaint processes that the citizen can go
through? What exactly are your training procedures?
Is the officer told that John Q. Citizen can do the
following things in making a complaint?

Chief Duarte:

That is one of the first things we tell them. Has
anyone from your office talked to the recruits, Herman?

Ombudsman Doi:

Yes. I have been there on a few occasions, and have
spoken to the recruits.

Professor Moore:

Herman, have you discontinued the practice of having someone from your office sit in on the hearings now?

Ombudsman Doi:

No, we have not. We have not had a complaint about police misconduct for many, many months now.

Chief Duarte:

Many complaints still come to us directly, over the telephone or personally. We investigate those.

Professor Wyner:

Is there a particular type of person who goes to the Ombudsman's office rather than come directly to you?

Chief Duarte:

No.

Ombudsman Walton:

Do you tend to get complaints from higher socio-economic groups, or lower?

Ombudsman Doi:

I think both. The most vocal ones are from the higher economic group.

Chief Duarte:

Both. A lot of the transients come in. When I say transients, I mean the hippie types, because we have a lot here.

Professor Anderson:

I wonder if Herman Doi would comment on his relationships with the other police departments in the State of Hawaii.

Chief Duarte:
Nobody complains on the other islands, you know--too small.

Ombudsman Doi:
We have had some complaints, but we have had no problems.

Professor Moore:
On the basis of your experience, Chief Duarte, would you recommend to other police departments that they at least suffer an Ombudsman's office gladly?

Chief Duarte:
I certainly would. I think it's a good thing. I feel very strongly about it, as I said. The police will have to open themselves up to public scrutiny if we expect to get the support, trust and confidence of the public. This has been our difficulty in the past. I think we have been very secretive, very ingrown and this has caused many of our difficulties. The Ombudsman is a step forward, a progressive step forward, I would say.

Professor Moore:
How do members of the public become aware of their opportunities to register complaints?

Chief Duarte:

We have done this in public information bulletins,
in the press and even the television people have publicized this.

Ombudsman Doi:

The usual process is that if the person doesn't know,
he will usually go and see the official in charge of
the division that gave him trouble. So, if he is
picked up by the bluecoats he'll go down to the
station, talk to the lieutenant, and the lieutenant
will send him up to the investigating unit.

Chief Duarte:

At every one of our Commission meetings that we have
every Wednesday--we have five Commissioners who are
lay people--all of these complaints are reviewed by
the Commission. With every report that we send
to the Ombudsman's office, copies are forwarded to
all of the Commissioners individually and they review
them individually. We had a meeting yesterday, and
we reviewed three complaints. I don't think any
of them emanated from the Ombudsman's office.
They were complaints that had been referred to us
directly. They'll review our reports and findings,
the disposition of the complaint, and if they concur
with the findings fine,and if they don't, they ask
questions regarding certain allegations and certain

dispositions that we made.

Professor Moore:
I asked you earlier about the additional staffing
that would help directly to respond to complaints
from the Ombudsman's office. Do you now have
additional help?

Chief Duarte:
We have one additional man and we are asking for
another.

Professor Moore:
What about the additional time consumed on the part
of the force generally? For example, you mentioned
the practice of having them get the names and
addresses of witnesses so that that information will
be available in the event of a complaint. Has there
been an increment in the burden on the force more
generally?

Chief Duarte:
No, I don't think so. I think it just creates
an awareness that this is necessary, and it is
necessary whether we have a complaint or not,
to help us in court. The recommendation from
the Ombudsman helped us in this regard: We became
more conscious and aware that this was a necessity,
and we urged the men to do this. It is an additional
benefit, really.

Because it reaches beyond the complaint processing function and effects Department procedures.

Discussion

Professor Wyner:

What if the Governor developed an antagonistic, hostile attitude toward the Ombudsman and he wrote a memorandum to the department heads that said, "Do not cooperate with the Ombudsman."

Mr. Kaye:

He would be violating the law. But he might say, "I want to hear personally from you on every request for information you get."

Professor Wyner:

I was trying to set up an extreme situation in which the Governor really tried his best to put a million road blocks in the way of the Ombudsman. I ask this in a hypothetical way. Is it possible for the department heads to prevent all their employees from cooperating with the Ombudsman?

Director Kondo:

I think so, certainly.

Professor Wyner:

That could set the scene for quite a major clash?

Director Kondo:

Certainly.

Professor Moore:

In contrast with that hypothetical situation, the Ombudsman has a subpoena power to secure information if a department is reluctant to supply it, but he has never had occasion to do that.

Professor Wyner:

What if the Governor said that anything you sent to the Ombudsman goes through his office first? Would this in any way give the Governor more control over the kinds of replies you give to Mr. Doi? Is that a serious kind of action on his part-- I say serious because the Governor and his top staff people see a million people and do a million things. Would it really be a meaningful kind of control?

Director Kondo:

Yes. It would be as meaningful as he wanted to make it.

Professor Anderson:

But don't your questions imply that really this office cannot function without cooperation?

Professor Wyner:

Well, that's what I'm driving at, because in many other places where Lt. Governors or Mayors or whatever have set up these offices by executive order, the very existence of the office is often at the whim of the chief executive.

Ombudsman Doi:

I don't think they can shut off information entirely,
forever, but they can shut off information for a
long time, making it very difficult for us to
operate.   There are many things they don't have to
tell us.   They can play games with us.   They can be
very evasive if they want to, and not answer the
question that is posed, give you all kinds of
trouble, and really make your life miserable.

Professor Anderson:

What this emphasizes is that Herman Doi does have
the cooperation, and I think had a great deal
initially and has only enhanced it.   The problem is,
you have to build up that confidence, which is obviously
what we have been talking about in terms of having
conferences with directors and other public servants.
In Nebraska, again, I suppose that is the first
task of the Ombudsman, and that is why he needs
some reservoir of public repute--which I was
pleased to read in a recent press release that he has.
Similarly, the method of choosing the Seattle
Ombudsman gives him an initial authenticity.   But
that is a very small checking account, and from
that he has to make the deposits and build it up,
before he has a sufficient reserve to be confident
of its continuance.

Chief Duarte:

A lot depends, too, on the personality of the man
selected as Ombudsman.

Professor Moore:

What that does is to eliminate an initial barrier to
understanding, where it becomes a question of
personality rather than a question of function.

Professor Anderson:

At our first meeting we tried to at least establish
that there are a variety of different personalities
and backgrounds, that nonetheless there are also
some people who would not be suited for this kind
of work.

Senator Schmit:

One man came to me wanting to be the Nebraska Ombudsman.
One of the reasons he felt he could do a good job,
he said, was that he was a born scrapper.

Ombudsman Walton:

Chief Duarte, if someone other than Herman had been
appointed, would it have made a major impact in your
approach or your attitude? The apprehension of the
department was there. Supposing somebody else had
been appointed, somebody you did not know?

Chief Duarte:

I did not know Herman at all. I knew of him, but I
did not know him personally.

Ombudsman Walton:
But if you can conceive of a situation where you
literally had a stranger there, would your attitude
have really been that much different?

Chief Duarte:
I think so, depending on the man that was selected.

Director Kondo:
Possibly the Ombudsman's office is a success partly
because many of the department heads are so young.
I don't know how important that is--young and more
adaptable to change.

Professor Moore:
It is true that one of the principal problems to
which an Ombudsman must address himself is not
deliberate maladministration,but rather the kind
of conventions thàt develop--habits, routines--and
he needs to be able to dislodge them. I think you
are quite right, it's easier to dislodge them when you
are dealing with people who are young either in
age or in mental set, than it is when you are
dealing with people that have been in that job for
years and are set in their ways.

Chief Duarte:
I'd like to add that it's easy to be a good guy
and get along with everybody, but Herman hasn't been
"the good guy." He has been very persistent.

I appreciate his persistency and the fact that he asserted himself.

Professor Moore:
He hasn't crossed the line to harassment?

Chief Duarte:
No, he hasn't harassed us.

Director Kondo:
That is a good point--being persistent and not harassing us. That is a very thin line. You start harassing me, and I am not going to cooperate.

Chief Duarte:
We would resist it if he harassed us. I am sure we would.
(Exit Chief Duarte and Director Kondo)

Ombudsman Walton:
How many of the 15 police complaints were dropped as simply unproved?

Ombudsman Doi:
In five or six cases there were only two persons involved, the officer and the person assaulted, in which we really could not make a case.

Professor Anderson:
Do you get any repetition of complaints against a single office or anything like that?

Ombudsman Doi:
In fact, we check the records to see if that particular

226

officer had been involved in any kind of fracas like that before, which might help in substantiating the position of the complainant. But, in most of the cases the persons who were cited were commended in the past for their behavior.

EVALUATING THE FUNCTIONS AND IMPACT
OF OMBUDSMAN OFFICES:
ROUNDTABLE

A G E N D A

Evaluation Design

I.   General Statistical Impact of Office

     A.   Number of complaints

     B.   Type of complaints

     C.   Resolution of complaints

     D.   Administrative Recommendations

     E.   Administrative Changes

     F.   Satisfaction of clients

     G.   Attitude of other generalized complaint
          handling offices

     H.   Public attitude toward government and
          awareness of office

II.   Analysis of Data

     A.   Relative success in identifying and
          rectifying justified grievances

     B.   Relative success in accomplishing improve-
          ments in government administration

     C.   Relative success in attracting and resolving
          the complaints of the poor

Professor Anderson:
We have distributed an agenda derived from OEO's

draft Evaluation Design. Roman I, General

Statistical Impact of the Office, is of course the

factual material that you will accumulate to use as

a basis for analysis. Obviously, you need to know

what kind of analysis you want to do--as Herman

Doi said at the beginning of the conference--

before you can know what kind of data you want to

gather.

RECORD-KEEPING

We have talked off and on about record-keeping,

and I don't think it would hurt just to run through

this list, to see if Lee Walton or Liem Tuai or

Loran Schmit have any questions, as they are the

ones that are going to be facing the problem of

setting up a bookkeeping system for an Ombudsman

office.

Devising Suitable Categories

We will be drawing again on the resources of the

Hawaii Ombudsman office to comment on any problems

that may be implicit in this particular list. For

example, in connection with the number of complaints,

item A, what is a complaint? Herman Doi makes it a

point to separate off inquiries so that his statistics

show whether something is genuinely a complaint or

whether a person is just asking for some kind of
information. This will be important for getting
uniformity of records, so that what one Ombudsman
puts down in his annual report will be comparable
to what another one does. I cannot think of any
other pitfalls involved in this category, but I
am sure you have a gray area: Sometimes you may
not know where to draw the line between an inquiry
and a complaint.

Professor Moore:
Didn't you recently redefine somewhat the category
of nonjurisdiction? What was the change?

Ombudsman Doi:
During the first year what we did was to categorize any
inquiry or anything involving a nonjurisdiction
agency under the no-jurisdiction category. We found
that was inadequate to explain what was happening, so
what we did was to segregate out those inquiries
which were really informational inquiries and
we stuck them in the information category and
now no-jurisdiction are complaints about an
agency which does not fall in our jurisdiction. If
it is an informational inquiry about an agency that
does not fall within our jurisdiction, it's
included as an information inquiry. So our statistics
have changed somewhat.

We are doing it manually now, and it's driving us
up the wall--even drawing the line between the
various kinds of inquiries and keeping track of
them. What you want to show is the number of
inquiries that are really information seeking kinds,
and these should take you much less time to satisfy
than a complaint does.

Professor Moore:
On types of complaints, Herman, have you kept
those pretty much congruent with the subject matter
of the agencies involved, or have you used general
functional categories that might cut across
several agencies?

Ombudsman Doi:
We are still in the process of evolving our index
for complaints. In our subject index we have all
no-jurisdiction cases, all information cases and all
complaints. But, to assign appropriate subject
headings, to be consistent, is very difficult. That
is the most difficult file to keep up. But it is
important, in that you can always go back to a
like case in the past and be sure that you are not
changing your position in any way. What we have
been doing is relying mostly on memory at the
present time.

Professor Anderson:

We should have a uniform nomenclature, so that all
like cases--whatever the subject matter--will be
recorded the same way in different offices,
recognizing that you are always going to have
some gray areas.

We need a coding system, then, so that the data can
be punched on a card and used either as a handwritten
or typewritten ledger system, or on an IBM or other
data processing system. You have not developed a
number system, have you? There have been other
jurisdictions that have developed a numbering system
to help them find a given case. It starts out with
the year as the first identifying number, then a
number which indicates the agency, then a number
which indicates the simple sequence of cases from
that agency. It isn't really too helpful, as
it is only a substitute for writing the name of
the agency and the year. I think we need something
a little more refined than that.

Professor Moore:

Herman, you have someone working on this?

Ombudsman Doi:

Yes. It is mostly to extract the kind of data that
we have already set out in blank tabular form. So,
it is a rather simplified system. We have not found

232

a good solution to our subject index file yet.
We have been starting from the index of Hawaii Revised
Statutes, on the basis that practically every
case would fall into one of these legal subject
indexes. That table is so long that it is
not very useful, so we really have to cut it down.

Professor Moore:
Moreover, that would make it difficult to compare,
say, Nebraska and Hawaii, if it was based upon
statutes peculiar to Hawaii. Using automatic
data processing may alleviate some of these problems
of categorization. Cross-filing becomes much
easier, because a machine does it.

Professor Wyner:
You still have to make those hard choices.

Professor Moore:
However, you do eliminate the mechanical part of it,
for example deciding how much cross-indexing you are
going to do.

Ombudsman Doi:
I think what John is talking about is that you can
start with much broader subject headings and have
a good cross index file to be able to locate the
specific case that you want.

Appraising the Resolution of Complaints

Professor Anderson:

Resolution of Complaints, Item C, is a tough one, especially to get uniformity. There is a good deal of subjectivity here in terms of appraisal, and this is the initial step of self-appraisal, because you are saying, did I have a successful resolution of this complaint, was it rectified, as some people would put it, or justified, as others would call it?

This can sometimes be a matter of opinion. Let me give an example. In New Zealand, the Ombudsman has been reluctant to record rectification of justified complaints from prisoners in penitentiaries. After he settles the matter, he has the prisoner withdraw the complaint, and then it is recorded as withdrawn. He does not want to project an image of taking the side of prisoners against guards. His motives may just be to keep down the flow of complaints--that is not to publicize it among prisoners, although he may not be successful in that. As we all know, prisoners' grapevines are very effective. Secondly, he seems to feel that this is not an agency where it would be helpful to have public identification of this sort of thing. I think personally that there are overwhelming considerations

in the other direction, and that he should treat all
of them alike. Maybe that is not the best example,
because it is so extreme.

Professor Moore:
But it does point out the really delicate problem
here of trying to obtain comparable data, because
this is so integral a part of the whole style of a
particular Ombudsman: whether he decides, as
Herman has done, to encourage voluntary rectifications,
or whether he thinks in his particular setting it is
more important to establish the vigor of the office in
the public mind by saying that the agency acceded
to the recommendation of the Ombudsman office.

Professor Anderson:
I would think that this system of indicating
voluntary rectification is a good idea. It
impresses everyone with the reasonableness of the
office, that you are not cramming solutions down
people's throats, that most of the time it is
done by mutual concurrence.

Ombudsman Doi:
There is a psychological factor involved, too.
In the course of negotiations with the administrator,
often it is a great incentive for him to accept
the recommendation on the basis of our saying, "Look,

why don't you suggest the action that we have been
talking about, and we will classify it a voluntary
rectification?"

Mr. Kaye:
What are the specific categories of resolution that
you have?

Ombudsman Doi:
We have "change in procedure," "change in regulation,"
"change in statute," "disciplinary action"...

Professor Anderson:
..."voluntary action," which is where the bulk come
in, and then "action not necessary," which is the
other main category.

Professor Wyner:
Are these mutually exclusive categories?

Professor Anderson:
I think they would be.

Professor Wyner:
How about the category "voluntary rectification?"

Professor Anderson:
Maybe the word voluntary isn't quite the best word.
Maybe what we are saying, and what you said earlier,
Herman, was that at least technically the suggestion
for it came from the agency. I mean in a sense you could
make the recommendation and they could still accept

it voluntarily rather than your having to go to the Legislature or to the press or get into a big hassle with them. I mean, don't they accept your recommendations, even though they come from you, "voluntarily?"

Ombudsman Doi:
When we cannot get resolution in the informal conference, then we do send them a formal letter of recommendation.

Professor Anderson:
It seems to me that what may be involved here is a question of timing. For example, when the New Zealand Ombudsman sends a complaint to the top administrator in an agency, he often finds that even before or simultaneously with the report back to him of the facts, they have already done something. He then indicates that the complaint was rectified before he made any recommendation or made any finding of facts. Maybe our references to voluntary compliance should reflect the time when the agency took corrective action: at the time of notice, at the time of the determination of the facts, or whether it precedes the recommendation of the Ombudsman. Voluntariness in all these areas is a little bit ambiguous, and there is some pressure

at the point when you send that first letter which
you cannot say is completely voluntary. If they had
not heard from you, they might have chosen not to
do anything.

Categories D and E relate to the consequences of the
action--administrative recommendations and
administrative changes. Naturally, you are going
to record those and they won't be that frequent as
compared to your total case load.

Herman Doi also records statutory changes. I think
that is a good thing to keep a record of, too.
If the Ombudsman were to recommend that disciplinary
action be taken in an agency in accordance with
normal procedures, that is also something you would
want to record.

Determining the Sources of Complaints

Ombudsman Walton:
I assume you would be interested in the source of
the complaints, for instance, by referral.

Miss Stolfa:
Is there a referral section?

Professor Anderson:
Herman, do you keep records on referrals?

Ombudsman Doi:

We do informally. We have no place on our present form.
We are planning to put in a space. But, we do not
make a practice of asking the guy whether or not he was
referred. If he mentions it during the course of
a complaint, then we will note it.

Ombudsman Walton:

The other thing is sociological information--to
the extent it is available, you would be interested in
it, I suppose.

Professor Anderson:

Yes, but again you don't ask him. What we have done
in Iowa is just to ask the Ombudsman or the individual
that speaks to the complainant to make a commonsense
judgment, "Is this a poor person?" Just to make
that one observation--more than that you can't
really do because your primary job is to help people
with their complaints not to interview them for
social science reasons.

Ombudsman Doi:

The more questions you ask the inquirer, the harder
it is to get the complaint. This has been our
experience here. Some people don't even want to give
their name, address and phone number.

Ombudsman Walton:

You could not ask for this kind of information. It is
a question of whether you can acquire it...

Professor Anderson:

The Ombudsman is characterized by a low threshold
of access.

Senator Schmit:

A guy with a grievance wants to get on the phone and
talk to the Ombudsman, and not have to answer
15 questions on who his wife is and where he lives.
They want to tell you about their complaint--bang--
and get you to do something about it quickly.

Professor Anderson:

The way that Herman works with the telephone and with
letters, he makes sure that he has the facts right
and establishes that the person does exist. This
they can understand.

We seem to agree then that you should get the name
and address and telephone number, and that is about it--
nothing more.

Ombudsman Doi:

If you can get that much, you are doing fine.

Senator Schmit:

We are trying to cut red tape, not build it. We
should not reach the point where we build up a biography
of each complainant.

Ombudsman Ealton:

I think that ultimately the Ombudsman should be prepared
to come up with solutions that prevent problems from

happening. And partly he needs to know the
clientele, the kinds of people, their patterns
of problems, so that these problems can be solved,
cut off along the line. You cannot do this
unless you are able to analyze the data, not by
infringing on the person, but by using statistical
methods.

Professor Anderson:
We should have a good deal of information about the
kind of complaint and the agency involved that will
be useful in doing what you suggest.

Measuring and Obtaining the Timely Disposition of Complaints
Mr. Douglas:
One statistical measure you might want would indicate
the time lag in resolving complaints.

Ombudsman Walton:
Do you keep track of the amount of time spent on
an individual case?

Ombudsman Doi:
We are not keeping that kind of statistic. Some
of my research assistants are beginning to note the
number of contacts in rough figures, the amount of
time that they have spent on that case.

This is not going to be a very significant statistic,
in the sense that the analyst who is working on

the case will be working on about 20 or 30 cases.
So, the amount of time he devotes to any individual
case is going to vary tremendously. But it is a
good statistic in the sense of finding out, on the
average, how long the complaint takes to handle, how
long does the information inquiry take, and how long
does a no-jurisdiction case take.

One other statistic that is important is the
amount of time that elapses from when you contact
the department to when you get a response.

Mr. Douglas:
Do you have any standards of how fast a complaint
must be handled?

Ombudsman Doi:
If there is a time lag between the complaint coming
in and the time you get the response from the
department, you are going to have to keep that complainant notified that you are still handling his
complaint, that you have not received a response.
We have not placed any time limits on our analysts.
They use their own judgment on when it is necessary
to contact a client again.

Professor Moore:
You have a reminder system, don't you? It might be

useful to beginning ombudsmen to make clear to the
agency people that this is going to be normal practice,
that reminders will be sent. You do not want to
offend these people, but you do want to make it clear
that you expect a fairly prompt response, and
if you put it in terms of your own housekeeping needs,
you might be able to make your expectation less
offensive.

Ombudsman Doi:
We started very optimistically by notifying the
departments that we would like to hear from them
either by phone or in writing within a period of one
week, but that is impossible for the departments
to comply with. So, now we are about at two weeks,
I think.

Ombudsman Walton:
You can't expect them to drop everything.

Ombudsman Doi:
We use a reminder. By sending a copy to the complainant,
                                              not
he knows we have not forgotten him, but we do/have
to send him a second letter. Where the transaction
is by phone, the analyst is responsible for contacting the complainant and advising him that we still
have his complaint in hand.

243

Professor Anderson:
As I recall, all the new cases from the previous week are discussed at a meeting by you and all of your staff on the following Monday. Does that mean that no letter can get out on a case until the following week?

Ombudsman Doi:
No. As soon as the complaint is received, the analyst will look at the case and draft an initial letter of inquiry. It will come across my desk at that time. Usually, within one or two days after the complaint is received, the first letter goes out.

Professor Anderson:
So that letter is the basis for your Monday discussion, really.

Ombudsman Walton:
That letter of inquiry, couldn't it simply be a buck form, simply attaching the allegation from your original copy? Is it necessary to prepare a new letter of request?

Ombudsman Doi:
We thought about using forms, when we started, but I don't think a form carries as much weight as a personal letter, and that is the reason why we went to magnetic Selectric card typewriters. That is the most efficient way to get correspondence out.

244

Ombudsman Walton:
How does that work?

Ombudsman Doi:
Well, you dictate the letter, the secretary transcribes
it, it is recorded on a magnetic card at the time
she is typing the draft. She types the draft, it goes
back to the analyst who corrects the letter, it comes
across my desk, I correct it, it goes back to the
typist. Then, she corrects the card only in places
where we have made corrections on the draft. Then she
replays the card and the letter comes back in corrected
form.

Mr. Douglas:
Do you ever make a phone call before you send these
first letters?

Ombudsman Doi:
Many times, to find out more about the case so you can
ask intelligent questions in your letter of inquiry.

Mr. Douglas:
What if someone comes in with a relatively minor
problem?

Ombudsman Doi:
We use the phone. We make a distinction between
the more complex and the really simple ones.
In a simple case we just use the phone; we don't
send the letter. In a complex case we use the

letter form. This is a judgmental decision that the staff members make initially upon receipt of the complaint.

Professor Moore:
Wasn't one of the principal feedbacks that you received from the agency heads, that they preferred the phone?

Ombudsman Doi:
They prefer that we use the phone much more than we do letters. It takes time for them to prepare a written response.

We have a separate piece of paper called "Notes to File" which the analyst is supposed to fill out for every phone call he makes.

Satisfaction of Clients

Professor Anderson:
This is a tough one. You don't want to call the guy up and say, "Oh, what did you think of what we did for you?" Yet, this is information that I think would be valuable to your office. Have you had any complaints from your customers?

Ombudsman Doi:
Sure we have.

Professor Anderson:
How do they come to you?

Ombudsman Doi:

One came by way of a letter-to-the-editor of a
newspaper. Some people have gone back to their legislators, because they ask us, "Where can I go to complain
about the Ombudsman?" I tell them, "Please go and
see your legislators. They are the people who appointed
me."

Professor Anderson:

What about compliments? Do you ever get any people
who take the trouble to contact you when it is over?

Ombudsman Doi:

Yes, we have had quite a number of letters. Those
whom you help will probably be the people who will
write to thank you for what you have done. Those
you found the complaint to be unjustified in most
cases will feel that you have not been of help.
They are not going to be very satisfied.

Ombudsman Walton:

It looks like a postcard survey is going to be
helpful.

Professor Moore:

I was wondering if you could comment on that, Herman.
I am thinking about our discussion of the imposition
on the complainant that would be involved in seeking
more data than name, address and telephone number.
Do you think that if you gave them a card and asked
them to fill it out that they would think that this

is just another bit of paper for another bureaucratic agency?

Ombudsman Doi:
I get cards from companies that sell products about the quality of their product, and this kind of thing. I don't think it gives you an accurate measurement of satisfaction. The guy could care less how he fills out that card after he is through; he will probably not send it back.

Professor Moore:
We are trying postcards in Iowa to see what kinds of responses we will get.

Professor Anderson:
What you are faced with is that anybody who either criticizes or compliments you is one of a self-selected group, and you are curious about all the others, the majority, who don't do one thing or the other. That would be nice information for you to have. With the postcard you are still getting a self-selected group: it is only those who take the time and trouble to fill it out and send it in, so you have only made the self-selected group a little bit larger.

Ombudsman Doi:
I think you are going to find that the returns are going to be very small.

Ombudsman Walton:

The postcards might be more effective if they were

signed by, and returned to, someone like the

President of the City Council, rather than the

Ombudsman. Secondly, wouldn't you get a more valid

sample by having somebody occasionally make a

random telephone survey? You would eliminate the

extremes.

Professor Anderson:

Theoretically, it could be 100%. There would

simply be a follow-up call, when the case was closed,

to check with the person to see if they were

satisfied that everything had been done that could

be done, or something like that. I suppose that

would be unnecessary and burdensome.

Ombudsman Walton:

Yes, if you are dealing with hundreds, it could be

done, but not for thousands. I think you have to go

with a random kind of sampling--which I think statistica-

lly is just as valid. You can get just as much

information from 10 or 20% as you can from 100%.

EVALUATION

How Are They Doing?

Professor Anderson:

To put this on a more general level, we are talking

now about appraising Ombudsman offices, and of course

the satisfaction of the clients is only one measure

249

of that. Now we are beginning to reach something
that we in the Ombudsman Activities Project are
struggling with, prodded now and again by the
Office of Economic Opportunity, because they would like
to know, too, how well their money is being spent.
This is a general problem. Some governmental agencies
or private industries have a fixed product, and can
compile a profit-and-loss statement. For others, you
can have some kind of efficiency analysis. You
could do an efficiency analysis on an Ombudsman
office--the extent to which people are active and
productive. But, how do you measure the success
of this office?

Professor Moore:
Perhaps we could ask Senator Kawasaki to comment on
that. From the legislator's standpoint, Senator, what
would you consider to be evidence of success as far
as an Ombudsman office is concerned?

Senator Kawasaki:
I suppose a lot of these criticisms and commendations
have been directed to me, because I was involved in
sponsoring the bill. I receive a good number of
compliments on the way the Ombudsman office has
handled complaints directed to that office. I get
the impression that Herman's office is doing a good

job because of the number of comments made to me.

Professor Moore:
Doing a good job in what way, though? In solving
problems, or being nice?

Senator Kawasaki:
Being attentive enough to listen to the complaint.
Secondly, the fair manner in which you handled it.
Thirdly, the very fact that you replied by letter as
to what judgment you came to after your investigation
of the complaint. I have had nothing but compliments
so far as Herman is concerned. I have also read
some of the letters-to-the-Editor complimenting you,
and one that was critical of your office.

This year, when your office testified before some
of our committees, we appreciated that--your testifying
in favor of taxpayer or consumer-oriented bills.
Your opinion is of value to us. Of course, it gives
weight to the feasibility of enacting legislation.
Apart from statutory amendments you may recommend, I
think perhaps you should look into the area of recommend-
ing new pieces of legislation to improve the processes
of government.

Herman also testified in my Government Relations Committee on some county bills.

251

Ombudsman Doi:

Those were the ones that we recommended.

Senator Kawasaki:

They were helpful. As a member of the legislature, as
a member of a committee, I appreciate the fact that
your recommendation gives weight to the feasibility
of passing a bill. But, in general, I can judge
the effectiveness of this office by the informal
comments made to me, letters sent to me, and the
telephone calls received by my office.

Professor Moore:

That is an interesting addition to the kinds of
contributions that the office may make. You just
noted the value of their expert testimony in
support of more general legislative proposals, not just
the corrective legislation that the office itself
has suggested.

I wonder if I could ask you essentially the same
question, Liem? What do you think the City and
County Councils will be looking for in determining
whether or not this office is doing its job?

Ombudsman Tuai:

I think that I would probably basically agree with
the Senator, that it would depend upon the feedback
you get. People are more prone to give you a negative

reply than they are to give you a positive one: if
it is something that may be controversial, you
receive a hundred letters against and maybe 5 or 10
for. If we receive extraordinary complaints, there
is something wrong. If we receive compliments, the
first thing I will be is highly amazed and suspicious.
But, I don't know, it is something I really can't
place my fingers on. My personal reaction would be
that in working with this I will get a feeling for how
well complaints are handled. I can't think of any
single criterion right now that I would say, "If
you achieve that, you have done a good job." If we
don't receive any complaints, I think it will have
been handled properly. If we receive complaints, then
we know definitely we have to take a look at the
program and see why we received these complaints.

Senator Kawasaki:
One manner in which we can assess the effectiveness of
the office is through the comments we receive from
department heads or agencies in the government itself.
They have accepted the suggestions for improvement
made by Herman's office.

Professor Anderson:
These are informal conversations?

Senator Kawasaki:

Private conversations. This kind of comment
by administrators and agency heads in the administration
itself is a measure of his effectiveness. Invariably,
they have commented that the office handled the matter
fairly.

Ombudsman Doi:

John went through our case files when he originally
came to our office. I think this is a valuable index
of whether or not the office is doing what it is
supposed to do, and I think it is the only way you
are going to find out whether it is doing what
it is supposed to do.

Professor Moore:

Yes, I asked Herman in connection with a number of
these cases why he stopped where he did, what some
of the overtones were. It gives you some sense of
both the way the office approached the case and of
the reaction of the complainant. Probably a more
accurate sense than you would get from a postcard.
It is not that onerous a job.

Ombudsman Doi:

You have to look at the individual case, and make a
judgment whether they are doing their job or whether
they are not doing their job, and this is one of the
things that is evident in Scandinavia, I think. The

Ombudsman there was saying that in disputed cases, where
legislators know of the case, they will ask the
Ombudsman specifically what the facts were and what
his reasoning was and how he disposed of the case
as an indication of how effective the office is.
They go through selected cases in their discussion of
the office.

I have one further practical suggestion. In attempting
to define what the measurements should be, I would
like to suggest that perhaps Stan and John can talk to--
for example, in Seattle/King County--can talk to the
councilmen of Seattle/King County to find out what
measures of effectiveness they think are appropriate.

Professor Moore:
I must have talked to at least 25 percent of the
Legislature here, and you are quite right. Given the
scale of the governmental system at the municipal
and county levels, you can be exhaustive--you can
talk to every member.

Ombudsman Doi:
I think it is just as important in Nebraska to find
out what the Nebraska Legislature thinks. Otherwise,
if our standards of measurement don't meet the
requirements of the legislators, it is going to be
completely useless.

Mr. Kaye:

But, Herman, don't you think there is also a parallel
need to see what the people themselves expect of it,
and see if there are any irreconcilable differences?

Ombudsman Doi:

I agree with you in theory a hundred percent, but how
are you going to find that out?

Mr. Kaye:

Well, that is the problem. That is a problem we are
going to have to work on. I think the interest in this
kind of a grievance handling mechanism comes from a
general, ill-defined or undefined feeling that
somehow or other the business or government has
gotten so out of touch with its reason for being--
and that is to develop people--that the people are
lost, and you get the feeling of alienation which
is the thing that seems to curse the whole society and
which has very bad effects all along the line.
What we are looking for is an institution that brings
the people back into a relationship with what is going
on.

Ombudsman Doi:

I think you will find, initially, that the complainants who come to you believe that your office
is there as an advocate for them. It takes a lot of
education to teach them that you are not there as an
advocate, but rather as an objective person looking at

the facts and making an independent determination as
to whether their complaint is or is not justified.
And, thirdly, I think it is just as important, once
having found the complaint is either justified or
unjustified, to explain the reasons why you made
that finding.

Professor Anderson:
I think the alienation point is well taken, although
the Ombudsman doesn't have to bear the whole burden
for attempting to make people feel more comfortable
with their government.

Ombudsman Walton:
Maybe the Ombudsmen are like the Courts. Ninety
percent of the people will never use it. Just
knowing it is there makes you feel more comfortable.

What Are They Doing?

Professor Anderson:
After we have kept the records, what kind of
inferences can we draw from them? In the past
couple of days several people have commented on the number
of complaints. For example, the gentlemen from the
Office of Information and Complaint pointed out
that when you do a good job of complaint-handling
you get more complaints, because people believe
that it is worthwhile.

But there must be some other factors and some

other limitations. Starting with the extremes, if
an Ombudsman office didn't get any, or didn't
get many complaints, you would figure there was
something wrong with its publicity, or that when
people took time to complain nothing had happened, and
after a while they stopped coming. If you get a
deluge of complaints, you have got to start looking
at the type of complaints, and if they are all cesspool
complaints, you know you are not running an Ombudsman
office, you are running an Office of Information
and Complaint. So from the number and type, you
would be able to make a judgment that this office
was or was not performing a proper Ombudsman function.

As far as a successful resolution is concerned, I
suppose we have seen a range of justified complaints
develop. Where the complaints are clearly
identified, Herman gets up to about 30% that are
justified. In other areas, where they may have
mixed in a lot of inquiries that are not really complaints, the percentage tends to be less. And we have
a range of experience from other countries. If you
got practically zero percent rectification, or if you
got up above 50%, we would begin to wonder if this
office was really performing its proper function.

Those would be red flags we would have to watch.

Ombudsman Walton:
You might have to establish a new standard, because you are dealing with local government.

Professor Anderson:
Well, we could go through all the Ombudsman reports in Scandinavia and in Canada for their local government work, because many of them do have local government jurisdiction.

Mr. Kaye:
We are talking in terms of numbers of complaints. But isn't there a sort of a mix that you have to be looking for--number and type. For instance, if you started off with a lot of complaints against the tax agency, and then they began to tail off...

Professor Anderson:
Yes, this would be a measure of improvement in administration at the same time. We know we are using complaints to measure the efficiency and propriety of what the agencies are doing. Now we are trying to figure a way also to use it to measure the effectiveness of the Ombudsman office. I appreciated Councilman Tuai's approach too. Just as injustice is often more easy to recognize than justice, I think this negative approach can be useful.

259

We have already made the value judgment--you
by passing the legislation, we by devoting our
time to study of this office of Ombudsman--that it is
basically valuable. So when we talk about evaluating
it, we are asking if there was something in the
particular office that was a weakness and perhaps enough
to make it a failure, or was the particular Ombudsman
simply unable to carry out his role, because he lacked
the qualifications that we discussed in the first
meeting?

Professor Moore:
Or was the setting such as to preclude the possibility
of any Ombudsman being effective?

Should They Be Doing It?
Mr. Kaye:
I am not so sure that you are right, though,   about
the value judgment. They made it in Hawaii, where
they went whole-hog and authorized the appropriations.
But for the OEO funded projects, I think, in a sense,
that it still has to be proven that this is a proper
function.

Professor Anderson:
Well, would you say that if they were as successful
as Herman Doi that it would then be proven?

Mr. Kaye:

Well, I might say it, but I wonder what the
Legislature in Nebraska is looking for...

Senator Schmit:

Could I comment here? I think you are painting
Nebraska with a brush that we don't deserve, because
Nebraska passed the legislation and then OEO came
to us and volunteered to fund it. I don't mean to
be critical, but in deference to Nebraska, we did
not pass a bill to take advantage of a federal appropriation.

Professor Moore:

Similarly, with Seattle/King County, while it is
true that Federal money undoubtedly facilitated action,
it is clear that the people there were looking ahead
two years. They were thinking about what the cost
to the city and county would be if, having established
this office and run it for two years, they were then
going to have to continue funding it. So they
didn't just take the money and say, "Well, we will play
with it for two years and not worry about what we will
do later."

Councilman Tuai:

It will be a consideration. We did start working on it,
but we were not going very fast until OEO came in,
and that did give us the impetus to get off our duffs

and to really work at it. I think the concept was sold to most people because, as I indicated, the County had to have one--their Charter provides for one. So it was a question of whether or not it would be a joint Seattle/King County office.

There is no doubt in my mind that in a year, two years, three years, whatever it may be, that when we go back to the councils we are going to look at it pretty hard. I wouldn't want to mislead you on that. We do have the Office of Citizens' Complaints now, and I was telling Lee this morning that my pitch has been that we can probably eliminate most of the money going into that office. I know we can talk about going the other way too. I may be wrong on that, but with our financial situation in the City of Seattle right now, we cannot say "We will dig up another $60,000 more or $50,000 more." It may well be that we are going to have to combine these offices somehow in order to get the dollar savings when we go out on our own, but that is a couple of years hence...

Professor Anderson:
You can put them under the same roof, but you would have two quite different functions going. Well, if

I understand both Ira and Liem, I think there are
two possibilities that could lead to a repeal of a
going Ombudsman office. One would be that the office
has failed for whatever reason--improper man, improper
setting, improper structure of office. Or, it might be
a perfect success in Seattle, and people might say
it's really nice, but it is a luxury we can't afford.
So, ironically, Ira, the Office of Economic Opportunity
is not the one that has to make a final judgment.
You have already made a preliminary value judgment
that it was worth supporting, but your commitment
is limited in time. The test that is going to be
made of these Ombudsmen and of our study is going to
be, do they keep it? Do other states and cities come
in? Does it continue to work? You won't know the
final payoff of your investment for a decade or so.

Mr. Kaye:
We are not concerned that narrowly. Our concern would
be how we utilize the findings in order to either
encourage other jurisdictions, to use it or modify
it, or make an absolute judgment, "Well, this is
irrelevant to the poor and therefore OEO does
not have to do anything about it." But the thing
that concerns me is that having made our investment,
and wanting to see not only the poverty impact of the

Ombudsman either proven or disproven, but really
to see the institution grow--that we find a
methodology of establishing success.

Ombudsman Doi:
I think Ira has a very valid point in this sense,
that whatever the standards or measurements of
success are, I think there has to be agreement on
the part of those legislators who have the decision-
making powers as to whether it is going to be con-
tinued or not, as well as those who are studying
the project. Unless you have the same kind of
basis for judgment, I don't see how a firm decision
can be made. You people may say, "Oh, it is
successful," but if the legislators think it is a pile
of junk, it isn't going to work at all. I think
the standard of measurement has to be the same.

Professor Moore:
To reverse that situation, it might be that you get
a lot of popular acclaim and people think it is a
really groovy thing, but that in fact there is
very little to show for it in terms of substantive
accomplishment.

Ombudsman Doi:
In that case, John, I'd bet my money that it would
continue.

264

Professor Moore:
For the short run. It might go on for two or three years before it really registered that some people were making a big noise but the office was not really accomplishing much.

Ombudsman Doi:
Basically I am thinking about the experiment they had in Buffalo, New York, where OEO thought it was a good project, but it was never adopted after that.

Professor Anderson:
For political reasons.

Ombudsman Doi:
If that situation exists, then I think you have lost the whole impact of having the project--if it is not adopted by the councilmen or the legislators thereafter.

Professor Anderson:
Well, the only thing we salvage from it is the ability to present that experience to other places that might want to try it. In that particular case, there was a simple loggerhead between the political parties of the Council and the Mayor. When he was defeated, the Council just wasn't about to continue what the opposition party Mayor had tried to start.

Let me shift the discussion just a bit--and this
is a little selfish, because I am talking more about
one of the problems of a political scientist.
The grand theory of Ombudsmanry hasn't been devised.
We haven't worked the Ombudsman into the history
of political theory, the tremendous literature
going back to Plato and including, say, the
Federalist Papers. The political theorist who
will do that has not yet appeared. I think that
perspective will help us. We will then be able
to discuss the value of the office in the context
of a long history, and maybe the history is
essential before the theory so that we are not
talking in abstractions. Hopefully, as we
go along, we may be able to define this kind of
conceptual framework. We will be talking in
terms of democracy, participatory democracy,
responsiveness of government. These are words
we can use, but we don't have an intellectual
history comparable to that of our other, more
well-established political institutions.

But, on the other hand that is a delight and
a challenge. Instead of just hacking over the
old stuff, as people have been doing for decades,
we have something new to get our teeth into.

266

It seems to me that there are certain basic
minima of a democratic government under law.
Even in the straitest of circumstances, you are
not going to do away with your court system, and
simply have policemen put people in jail when they
seem to be getting in trouble. You have to have an
arbiter of civil disputes. I wonder if this
isn't as basic an institution as that--both the
complaint handling function on a crude basis--for
example, cesspools--and the more refined one which
looks at administrative procedure.

I wonder if our society hasn't developed from the
point where the courts were the crucial institution
to the point where we have got to get the equivalent
of these institutions in the administrative sphere.
It may not be a question of whether you want it
or not, or can afford it or not; you have to have
it, or something like it. Of course, you want it to
be as good as it can for as little as possible as
you do with the courts. But then you recognize
the inefficiency of having low-paid judges, and so
on, and the same thing would apply here, that
there is false economy in being parsimonious. I don't
say that I'm convinced that is the case, but I

think that may be the direction that our theorizing
is going to have to go.   Then it becomes a matter
of conviction, really.

Councilman Tuai:
I can't disagree with your theory, but I don't
think we have reached that maturity or sophistication
as yet, to say this is one of the things which is
as necessary as our health department or engineering
department.

Professor Anderson:
I agree with you.   I think we are still a primitive
society in many ways, and this is kind of a badge
of civilization.

One of the undeveloped constitutional rights is the
one that says that the right of the people peaceably
to assemble for the redress of grievances shall not
be abridged.   Really, this has been little applied.
You can interpret it in such a way that
it only means that anybody has a right to say something to someone else.   Maybe the proper theme of
analysis for the Ombudsman office should be this
relatively little used and interpreted section of the
Constitution of the United States--analogous to the
Supreme Court having invented the constitutional

right of privacy by finding it interstitially
located in a few other constitutional rights,
such as freedom from search and against self-incrimina-
tion, and so on.

It seems to me that we have reached a stage in
our constitutional growth where the government
is not simply, as it used to be, the preventor
of unconstitutional action--that is, when something
unconstitutional occurs, the courts will strike
it down and say you shouldn't have done this.
We have come to the point of positive implementation
of the Constitution. We have to actually go out
and seek its application, not just look for
governmental action violating it.

The Ombudsman office is such an implementation, making
the right of petition a real tool of the people,
and not just a forgotten line in the constitution.
The right to petition means that someone in the
government will listen to you, that he will maybe
gather further facts if necessary, that he will
reach a judgment in regard to your petition, and
perhaps recommend some action. Maybe the Ombudsman
is a constitutionally required institution in our
society. It may be a little while before the Supreme

Court reaches that judgment.

Professor Moore:
We have truly reached the outer limits of all
available authority, I suppose, if we conclude
that an Ombudsman is not only desirable, but is
required by the Constitution.

Professor Anderson:
You notice that I stopped short of making it
some sort of divine requirement.

NOTES

1. See Stanley Anderson, *Canadian Ombudsman Proposals* (University of California, Berkeley: Institute of Governmental Studies, 1966).

2. See Dean Mann, *The Citizen and the Bureaucracy: Complaint-Handling Procedures of Three California Legislators* (University of California, Berkeley: Institute of Governmental Studies, 1968).

3. See John Moore, "State Government and the Ombudsman," in Stanley Anderson, ed., *Ombudsmen for American Government?* (Prentice-Hall, 1968).

4. See Stanley Scott, ed., *Western American Assembly on the Ombudsman: Report* (University of California, Berkeley: Institute of Governmental Studies, 1968).

5. See Alan J. Wyner, "Lieutenant Governors as Political Ombudsmen," *Public Affairs Report* (University of California, Berkeley: Institute of Governmental Studies, December, 1971).

6. The first three Reports of the Citizens Administrative Service, Buffalo, New York, are found in Stanley Anderson, *Ombudsman Papers*, pp. 169-221. The CAS final report has been published as *Buffalo Citizens Administrative Service: An Ombudsman Demonstration Project* (University of California, Berkeley: Institute of Governmental Studies, 1970).

7. See *The Ombudsman* (University of Hawaii, Honolulu: Legislative Reference Bureau, mimeographed, November, 1965).

APPENDIX I

Record-Keeping Materials Supplied
by
Hawaii Ombudsman

.

C A S E   S T A T U S   R E P O R T

Analyst _____

Week Ending _____

Case No.	Dept.	Subject Matter	Date Complaint Rec'd.	Date of Initial Inquiry (method)	Dept. Response	Date Reminder Sent	What Has To Be Done Yet	Projected Date Closing Case

No._____

	Date		Taken by		Assigned to

Written ____   Phone Call ____   Visit ____   County _____

Name of
Inquirer_____   Phone_____ (R)

Address_____   _____ (B)

Type: No Jurisdiction ____   Information ____   Complaint ____

Subject:_____

Description:

Agency Involved:_____

	Phone	Letter			Phone	Letter
Date of Inquiry			Reply			
Subsequent			Subsequent			
Subsequent			Subsequent			

ACTION RECOMMENDED

Change in Procedure	Change in Regulation	Change in Statute	Disciplinary Action	Other

NO ACTION RECOMMENDED

Voluntary Rectification	No Action Necessary

Summary _____   Statutory Proposal _____

Comment:_____

_____

Justified or   Unjustified   Complainant Notified
Partially Justified

Date Closed:_____   Discontinued:_____

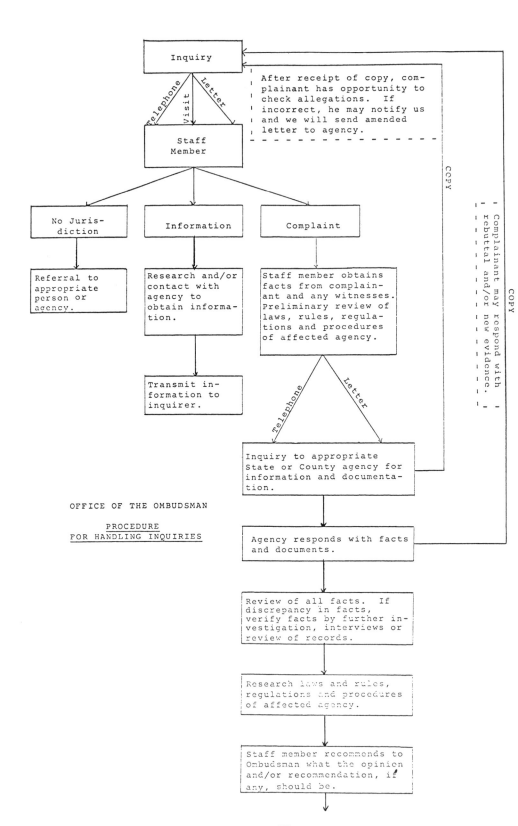

Inquiry

After receipt of copy, complainant has opportunity to check allegations. If incorrect, he may notify us and we will send amended letter to agency.

Telephone   Visit   Letter

Staff Member

No Jurisdiction

Information

Complaint

Referral to appropriate person or agency.

Research and/or contact with agency to obtain information.

Staff member obtains facts from complainant and any witnesses. Preliminary review of laws, rules, regulations and procedures of affected agency.

Transmit information to inquirer.

Telephone   Letter

Inquiry to appropriate State or County agency for information and documentation.

COPY

Complainant may respond with rebuttal and/or new evidence.

COPY

OFFICE OF THE OMBUDSMAN

PROCEDURE
FOR HANDLING INQUIRIES

Agency responds with facts and documents.

Review of all facts. If discrepancy in facts, verify facts by further investigation, interviews or review of records.

Research laws and rules, regulations and procedures of affected agency.

Staff member recommends to Ombudsman what the opinion and/or recommendation, if any, should be.

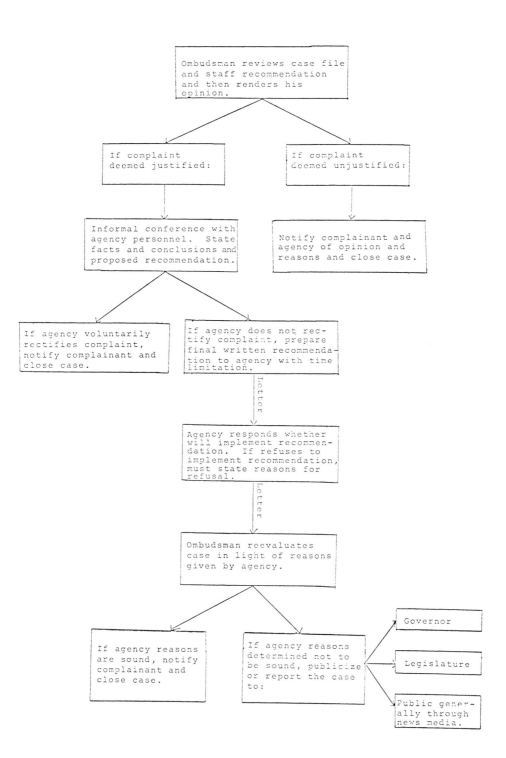

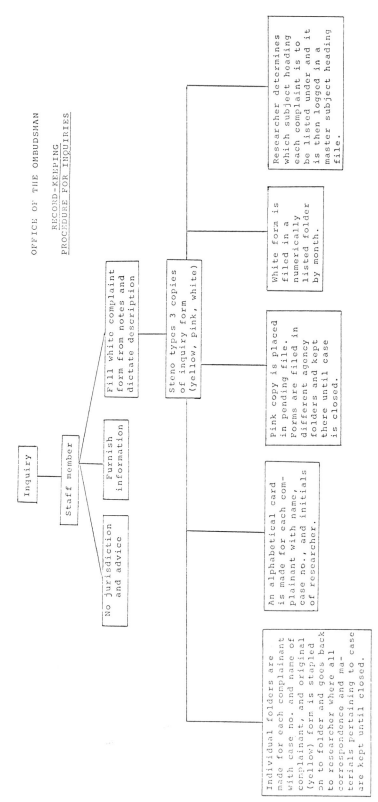

OFFICE OF THE OMBUDSMAN

RECORD-KEEPING
PROCEDURE FOR INQUIRIES

Inquiry

Staff member

No jurisdiction and advice

Furnish information

Fill white complaint form from notes and dictate description

Steno types 3 copies of inquiry form (yellow, pink, white)

Individual folders are made for each complainant with case no. and name of complainant, and original (yellow) form is stapled on to folder and goes back to researcher where all correspondence and materials pertaining to case are kept until closed.

An alphabetical card is made for each complainant with name, case no., and initials of researcher.

Pink copy is placed in pending file. Forms are filed in different agency folders and kept there until case is closed.

White form is filed in a numerically listed folder by month.

Researcher determines which subject heading each complaint is to be listed under and it is then logged in a master subject heading file.

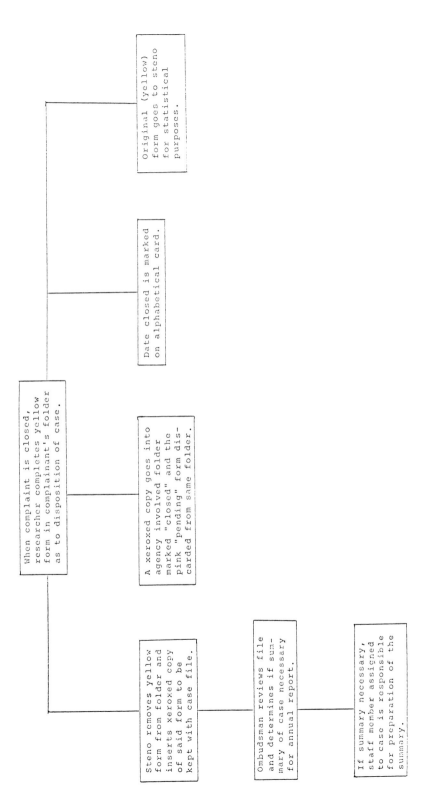

When complaint is closed, researcher completes yellow form in complainant's folder as to disposition of case.

Original (yellow) form goes to steno for statistical purposes.

Date closed is marked on alphabetical card.

A xeroxed copy goes into agency involved folder marked "closed" and the pink "pending" form discarded from same folder.

Steno removes yellow form from folder and inserts xeroxed copy of said form to be kept with case file.

Ombudsman reviews file and determines if summary of case necessary for annual report.

If summary necessary, staff member assigned to case is responsible for preparation of the summary.

TABLE 1
INQUIRIES
Number, Means of Receipt, Location, Type

Month	Total Inquiries	Means of Receipt			Location					Out of State		Type	
		Written	Visit	Phone	City & County	Hawaii	Maui	Kauai	No Juris-diction		Information	Complaint
July												
August												
September												
October												
November												
December												
January												
February												
March												
April												
May												
June												
TOTAL												
% of Total Inquiries												
% of Total Complaints												

Total - Male
        Female

279

TABLE 1A

INQUIRY REFERRALS

Type of Inquiry	Legislator	Congressional	State Officer or Employee	County Officer or Employee	Legal Aid	Attorney	Labor Organization	News Media	Other Persons
No Jurisdiction									
Information									
Complaint									

280

TABLE 2

DISTRIBUTION OF POPULATION AND INQUIRIES

County	Population and Percentage	Total Inquiries and Percentage	INQUIRIES		
			No Jurisdiction and Percentage	Information and Percentage	Complaints and Percentage
City and County					
Hawaii					
Maui					
Kauai					
Out of State					

TABLE 3

INQUIRIES FROM NEIGHBOR ISLANDS

	Total Inquiries	Long Distance Calls			Visits		
		No Jurisdiction	Information	Complaint	No Jurisdiction	Information	Complaint
Hawaii							
Maui							
Kauai							

TABLE 4

NO JURISDICTION EXCLUSION

Month	Courts or Cases in Court	Legislature Committees or Staff	Entity of Federal Government	Governor Personal Staff	Multi State Governmental Entity	Private Transactions
July						
August						
September						
October						
November						
December						
January						
February						
March						
April						
May						
June						
Total						
% of total						

Total Male:

Total Female:

TABLE 5
INFORMATION

State Departments,
Agencies or Miscellaneous | Totals

Accounting and General Services
Agriculture
Attorney General
Budget and Finance
Defense
Education
Hawaiian Home Lands
Health
Labor and Industrial Relations
Land and Natural Resources
Personnel Services
Planning and Economic Development
Regulatory Agencies
Social Services & Housing
Taxation
Transportation
University of Hawaii

Other Agencies
Lieutenant Governor
Consumer Protection
Hawaii Office of Economic Opportunity

Counties
City and County of Honolulu
County of Hawaii
County of Kauai
County of Maui

MISCELLANEOUS

TOTALS

% of Total
    Total - Male
            Female

TABLE 6

COMPLAINT DISPOSITION

Department or Agency	Total No. of Complaints	Complaints Investigated			Discontinued	At Close of FY Pending
		Justified or Partially Justified	Unjustified			
Accounting and General Services						
Agriculture						
Attorney General						
Budget and Finance						
Defense						
Education						
Hawaiian Home Lands						
Health						
Labor and Industrial Relations						
Land and Natural Resources						
Personnel Services						
Planning and Economic Development						
Regulatory Agencies						
Social Services & Housing						
Taxation						
Transportation						
University of Hawaii						
Other Agencies						
Lieutenant Governor						
Consumer Protection						
Hawaii Office of Economic Opportunity						
Counties						
City and County of Honolulu						
County of Hawaii						
County of Kauai						
County of Maui						
TOTALS						
% of Total						

Total Male:

Total Female:

TABLE 7

JUSTIFIED COMPLAINT DISPOSITION

Department or Agency	Justified or Partially Justified	Recommendation and Acceptance								Change in Statute	Voluntary Action by Department
		Change in Procedure		Change in Regulation		Disciplinary Action		Other			
		A	R	A	R	A	R	A	R		
Accounting and General Services											
Agriculture											
Attorney General											
Budget and Finance											
Defense											
Education											
Hawaiian Home Lands											
Health											
Labor and Industrial Relations											
Land and Natural Resources											
Personnel Services											
Planning and Economic Development											
Regulatory Agencies											
Social Services & Housing											
Taxation											
Transportation											
University of Hawaii											
Other Agencies											
Lieutenant Governor											
Consumer Protection											
Hawaii Office of Economic Opportunity											
Counties											
City and County of Honolulu											
County of Hawaii											
County of Kauai											
County of Maui											
TOTALS											
% of Total											

A = Recommended and Accepted
R = Recommended and Not Accepted

286

APPENDIX II

Text of Brochure,
Hawaii Ombudsman Office

(Text of Brochure)

LOCATION, OFFICE HOURS, AND PHONE NUMBERS

The Office of the Ombudsman is located in the Kana'ina Building (the old Attorney General's Building located on the Ewa side of the Library of Hawaii immediately in front of the Archives Building on the Iolani Palace Grounds). The address is:

Office of the Ombudsman
State of Hawaii
Kana'ina Building
Iolani Palace Grounds
Honolulu, Hawaii 96813

Office hours are 7:45 a.m. to 4:30 p.m. Mondays through Fridays. Telephone numbers are 531-0284 and 548-2811.

JURISDICTION AND ROLE

The Ombudsman's job is to investigate complaints from the public about executive departments of the State and County governments. Complaints about the following *will not* be accepted or investigated primarily because of statutory exclusion: (1) the governor and his personal staff; (2) the legislature, its committees, and its staff; (3) the mayors and councils of the counties; (4) the courts, including any action presently pending in the courts of this State or an action where a decision has been given or judgment rendered; (5) an entity of the federal government; (6) a multistate governmental entity; and (7) private companies, businesses, or persons, or other nongovernmental employees.

The Ombudsman *is not* an advocate of the complainant but rather an objective intermediary who reviews the facts of an incident to determine whether or not governmental administrators have acted or refused to act reasonably. If governmental administrators have not acted or refused to act reasonably, the Ombudsman may express his opinion and recommend corrective actions.

COMPLAINTS

Complaints may be brought to the attention of the Ombudsman by telephone, personal visit, or by letter. Members of the public should first contact the appropriate agency regarding their complaint, and if unsatisfied with the result, should contact this office.

Neighbor island residents will receive service from the Ombudsman by periodic visits. If you wish to phone in your complaint, call the office long distance collect and give our secretary your name, address, and phone number. We will call you back later through the State leased telephone lines. Periodic visits to the neighbor islands will also be made. If you wish to speak to someone from the office, call the District Superintendent for Education's Office in your county to arrange

for an appointment. The person to contact in the District Superintendent's Office is the superintendent's secretary. Their phone numbers
are as follows: Hawaii (Hilo vicinity)--Mr. Harry C. Chuck's secretary
at 961-7237; Hawaii (Kona vicinity)--Mr. Kenneth Asato's secretary at
329-1750; Kauai--Mr. Barton H. Nagata's secretary at 245-4493; and
Maui--Mr. Andy Y. Nii's secretary at 244-4221.

EMPLOYEE COMPLAINTS

Employees of the State and Counties should attempt to utilize the
internal grievance procedures before contacting the Office of the Ombudsman. In this regard, if you are a member of a union or association,
contact the union or association representative to assist you. If you
cannot resolve your complaint by using the internal grievance procedures, then contact the Office of the Ombudsman.

APPENDIX III

City and County of Honolulu
Office of Information and Complaint
Quarterly Report

January - March, 1971

WEEK OF	COMPLAINTS	INQUIRIES	SUGGESTIONS	ANNUAL RATE		
				COMPLAINTS	INQUIRIES	SUGGESTIONS
1- 4-71	78	65		4,056	3,380	
1-11-71	174	74	4	9,048	3,848	208
1-18-71	128	54	1	6,656	2,808	52
1-25-71	178	95	2	9,256	4,940	104
	558	288	7			
2- 1-71	178	86	1	9,256	4,472	52
2- 8-71	107	81	7	5,564	4,212	364
2-15-71	104	66	2	5,408	3,432	104
2-22-71	131	67	2	6,815	3,484	104
	520	300	12			
3- 1-71	102	146	3	5,304	7,592	156
3- 8-71	105	105	2	5,460	5,460	104
3-15-71	102	99		5,304	5,148	
3-22-71	98	73	1	5,096	3,796	52
3-29-71	169	99	2	8,788	5,148	104
	576	522	8			
TOTAL:	1,654	1,110	27			

TOTAL NO. OF:

WEEKS	13
COMPLAINTS	1,654
INQUIRIES	1,110
SUGGESTIONS	27

AVERAGE ANNUAL RATE:

COMPLAINTS	6,616
INQUIRIES	4,440
SUGGESTIONS	108

January - March, 1971

	January	February	March	Total	Req. Svc.	About Svc/Policy
AUDITORIUM		1	2	3		3
BOARD OF WATER SUPPLY	1		7	8	8	
Broken water lines	1		6	7	7	
BUILDING	38	40	31	109	106	3
Zoning violations - commercial	7	7	5	19	19	
Zoning violations - livestock	7	6	4	17	17	
Noise, constr'n/miscellaneous	4	6	7	17	17	
Building Code violations	7	4	4	15	15	
Zoning violations - trailer camps	6	2		8	8	
Signs, illegal		5	2	7	7	
CITY CLERK		1		1	1	
CORPORATION COUNSEL	8	7	3	18	16	2
Zoning violations - trailer camps	6	6		12	12	
Claims against City	2		2	4	4	
FINANCE	4	2	15	21		21
Auto vehicle registration	1	2	7			10
Licensing Division inefficiency			8	8		8
FIRE	4	1	5	10	10	
Fire hazards	3	1	4	8	8	
HAWAII STATE	5	17	17	39	38	1
Air pollution		3	7	10	10	
Consumer protection	2	1	3	6	6	
Mosquito control			5	5	5	
Health and sanitation	1	3	1	5	5	
HEALTH		1	5	6		6
Sirens, ambulance			3	3		3
HONOLULU REDEVELOPMENT AGENCY			3	3	2	1
LIQUOR COMMISSION	1			1	1	
MAYOR'S OFFICE	3		2	5		5
MODEL CITIES			2	2	2	
PARKS	26	34	26	86	38	48
Great Hawaiian Jubilee		13	1	14		14
Removal of City trees	6		8	14	14	
Bahana Store garden			10	10		10
Vandalism - City trees	7	1		8	8	
Tree trimming	1	6		7	7	
Park maintenance	2	4		6		6
PLANNING	7	7		14	12	2
Zoning violations-trailer camps	6	6		12	12	

	January	February	March	Total	Req. Svc.	About Svc/Policy
POLICE	50	60	72	182	145	37
Abandoned vehicles	10	16	32	58	58	
Illegal parking	3	12	9	24	24	
Police behavior/attitude	4	3	2	9		9
Cars towed	3	3	2	8		8
Barking dogs	7	1		8	8	
Noise, after-hour			6	6	6	
Noise, loud music	4	1		5	5	
Noise, construction	1	3		4	4	
Noise, police helicopter	3		1	4		4
Unfair traffic citations	4			4		4
Dust problem		2	2	4	4	
PRIVATE		8	2	10	8	2
PUBLIC WORKS	358	284	298	940	851	89
Engineering	76	40	82	198	188	10
Vacant lots, overgrown	9	13	21	43	43	
Flooding	29		7	36	36	
Drainage problems	15	7	8	30	30	
Sidewalks, damaged	2	5	9	16	16	
Illegal dumping in streams	5	2	5	12	12	
Sidewalk/roadway obstruction	4	3	6	13	13	
Manholes, open/loose covers	3	3	5	11	11	
Other sidewalk violations			11	11	11	
House numbering		6		6		6
Land Survey and Acquisition	3	6	6	15	14	1
Ownership title	2	5	3	10	10	
Lost boundary pins		1	3	4	4	
Refuse Collection & Disposal	160	121	127	408	348	60
Dead animals	71	66	98	235	234	1
Bulk item collection service	60	20	5	85	75	10
Refuse collection	16	13	8	37	35	2
Dump closure	2	4	3	9		9
Waianae refuse collection test	1	7		8		8
Street cleaning	3		4	7		7
Waipahu incinerator smoke	5	2		7		7
Refuse containers, damaged/lost		2	4	6		6
Road Maintenance	62	54	33	149	146	3
Road maintenance	45	44	26	115	115	
Drains, ditches, streams/maint.	16	6	7	29	29	
Sewers	57	63	50	170	155	15
Cesspool service	51	52	40	143	139	4
Sewage odor		7	3	10	10	
Sewer maintenance	3	2	1	6	5	1
TRAFFIC	50	57	86	193	171	22
Street lights out	14	12	13	39	39	
Mass transit (City buses)	6	11	39	56	36	20
Traffic signs/markings	16	13	6	35	35	
Traffic congestion/hazards	3	11	17	31	31	
Traffic signals	9	8	11	28	28	
U. S. GOVERNMENT	3			3	1	2
TOTAL	558	520	576	1,654	1,410	244